1-10

THE OPEN UNIVERSITY

An Arts Foundation Course
Unit 32

Twentieth - Century Responses to Industrialization

Prepared by Christopher Harvie, Charles Harrison and Graham Martin for the Course Team

The Open University Press

Cover Jacob Epstein Torso in metal from the 'Rock Drill', *bronze, 1913–16 (Tate Gallery Photo: John Webb)*

The Open University Press
Walton Hall, Milton Keynes
MK7 6AA

First published 1978

Designed by the Media Development Group of the Open University.

Printed in Great Britain by
EYRE & SPOTTISWOODE LIMITED
AT GROSVENOR PRESS PORTSMOUTH

ISBN 0 335 05424 2

This text forms part of an Open University course. The complete list of units in the course appears at the end of this text.

For general availability of supporting material referred to in this text, please write to Open University Educational Enterprises Limited, 12 Cofferidge Close, Stony Stratford, Milton Keynes, MK11 1BY, Great Britain.

Further information on Open University courses may be obtained from the Admissions Office, The Open University, P.O. Box 48, Walton Hall, Milton Keynes, MK7 6AB.

1.1

UNIT 32 TWENTIETH-CENTURY RESPONSES TO INDUSTRIALIZATION

CONTENTS

IMPORTANT NOTE

The television and radio programmes associated with this unit consist of television programme 32, a study of science fiction as a means of predicting the future of industrialization in the early twentieth century, and radio programme 32 *Life in a Railway Factory,* which looks at Alfred Williams, a steam-hammerman at Swindon Railway Works, who compared the rural life he had left with the organization and work-experience of a large industrial plant.

Television programmes 23 *Victorian* 29 *A Golden Age of Work* dealt in part with Ruskin's ideas and radio programme 25 *We War with Rude Nature* raises *Painting* and several of the themes we will be discussing.

You will need to consult the Course Reader, *Nature and Industrialization,* Alasdair Clayre (ed) (1977), Oxford University Press. You will also need to refer to the Colour Supplement and to the Supplementary Texts.

INTRODUCTION TO UNIT 32

After working your way through Units 21–31 in this extended case study you will, I hope, be conscious of some of the main political, intellectual and artistic debates raised by the experience of industrial change after the middle of the eighteenth century. Such issues include the political questions which turn on the division of the industrial spoils and the granting of new rights of citizenship and social control; the impact of new technologies, audiences and social situations on the techniques and subject matter of the creative arts, and, at a deeper level, the acquisition by significant groups in society, like women or the working class, of a new awareness or 'consciousness' of their social situation and the possibilities of remedying it.

Besides these issues, we have also uncovered a range of more fundamental if less straightforward questions, which hinge on the shift in man's relations with the natural world and with the historical past. Industrialization greatly enhanced his knowledge and control both of human personality and the resources of the natural world; but as well as liberating mankind from inherited superstition and constricting traditions this also defined his relations with the rest of nature as essentially exploitative, and imposed on societies throughout the world stresses and tensions which were to surface with explosive effect in the twentieth century.

The twentieth century has understandably been called 'the century of total war'. Certainly the two great wars have been dislocations as overwhelming in their consequences as industrialization was in the nineteenth century. Yet, thirty-three years after the end of the Second World War, many of the political and moral issues that social thinkers and creative artists raised in the nineteenth century have again become crucial. In this unit three of us attempt to discuss the contribution of social criticism, artistic theory and literature to such current questions by exploring the work of two individuals – the artistic and social critic John Ruskin and the novelist and poet D. H. Lawrence – and some of the pioneers of 'modernism' in the visual arts.

Christopher Harvie

PART 1 JOHN RUSKIN: IDEAS AND INFLUENCE
1 INTRODUCTION

When she read *The Stones of Venice* in 1851, Charlotte Brontë wrote to Mrs Gaskell: 'The *Stones of Venice* seem nobly laid and chiselled. How grandly the quarry of vast marbles is disclosed! Mr Ruskin seems to me one of the few genuine writers, as distinguished from book-makers, of this age.' Frederic Harrison (1831–1923) the radical critic, commented: 'A just and clear-sighted thought, worthy of *Jane Eyre,* with her way of seeing through outward show to the soul within the husk.' (Frederic Harrison, *John Ruskin,* page 69.) Charlotte Brontë's reputation, although rapidly acquired, has been sustained; Ruskin's, although comparable (roughly) until the period of the First World War, subsequently plummeted. As Lord Clark wrote in 1964 in his introduction to an anthology, *Ruskin Today*:

> Throughout the second half of the nineteenth century he was accepted by all thoughtful people as one of the impregnable figures of English literature . . . From Wordsworth to Proust there was hardly a distinguished man of letters who did not admire him . . . .
>
> Nor was his reputation confined to literature. Tolstoy, Gandhi and Bernard Shaw, to name only three, believed him to be one of the greatest social reformers of his time . . . When, at the first meeting of the Parliamentary Labour Party, members were asked what had been the determining influence on their lives, almost every one answered 'the works of Ruskin.'
>
> Now, in the middle of the twentieth century, what is left of this towering reputation? Practically nothing but a malicious interest in the story of his private life. (*Ruskin Today,* pp. xi–xii.)

So why begin a unit on nature and industrialization in the twentieth century with a Victorian writer whose popularity, once enormous, has not apparently been maintained? The quotations from Charlotte Brontë may explain Ruskin's historical significance, but has he any importance today?

Now one of the aims of this unit is to discuss recent criticisms of unchecked industrialization from both scientists and humanists: questions like the preservation of ecological balance and the 'exploitation' by the 'developed' world of the rest of the world's population and a disproportionate quantity of its natural resources. But you will find, if you explore these issues, that this criticism is continuous, from the Victorian period to the present. This section is the result of such an exercise. My case, which I have to prove to you, is that, of the various Victorian 'social critics' or 'sages' (see Units 24–25, *The Experience of Industrialization,* Section 14), John Ruskin had a unique influence – direct and indirect – on ideas about industrialization and culture. Moreover, Ruskin himself, idiosyncratic and perverse but capable of dramatic insights and vivid advocacy, personified a type of response which used the resources of religion and the arts to criticize the 'mechanistic' and 'materialistic' views of society and culture which were dominant in the first phases of industrialization. Part 1 of this unit deals, therefore, not with Ruskin's career as a whole, but with three of his key concerns: art, economics and nature. It surveys his ideas, their importance in his own age, and their significance today, both directly and by their effect on social action.

I give below the extracts from Ruskin's works which are printed in the Reader. You will be asked to read through some of them in the course of this section, and you may care to read, or re-read, all of them before you start.

Reference	*Passage*
III.3	'Turner's Childhood' from *Modern Painters,* 1860 edition
IX.2	'Rochdale and Pisa' from *Modern Manufacture and Design,* 1858
IX.3	'A city as it might be' from *The Mystery of Life and its Arts,* 1868

XVII.7	'The Nature of Gothic' from *The Stones of Venice,* 1851–3
XVII.8	'There is no wealth but life' from *The Veins of Wealth,* 1862
XX.1	'Millais and Turner' from *Pre-Raphaelitism,* 1851

2 LIFE AND ART

2.1 LIFE

John Ruskin was born in London in 1819, the son of a wealthy Scottish wine merchant (who did more than anyone else to make sherry a popular drink in Britain) and his wife, also of Scots descent. He was therefore, in our money, the son of a millionaire, and later a millionaire himself. He was also, in speech and many aspects of his mind, 'a Scot of Scots'. His upbringing was, characteristically, a severe Calvinist one, but his father was also a connoisseur, who, with wife and only child, travelled widely on the continent, and mixed in artistic society. He was wealthy enough to purchase for his son the education of a 'gentleman commoner' at Christ Church, Oxford (1836–42) where Ruskin studied both the classical curriculum and, unofficially, art and natural history. Not long after, he burst into print (anonymously) with the first volume of *Modern Painters* (1843), a passionate defence of the art of J. M. W. Turner. Despite its author's youth this gained enormous popularity and was steadily expanded, until it ran into five volumes. Charlotte Brontë wrote of it: 'I feel now as if I had

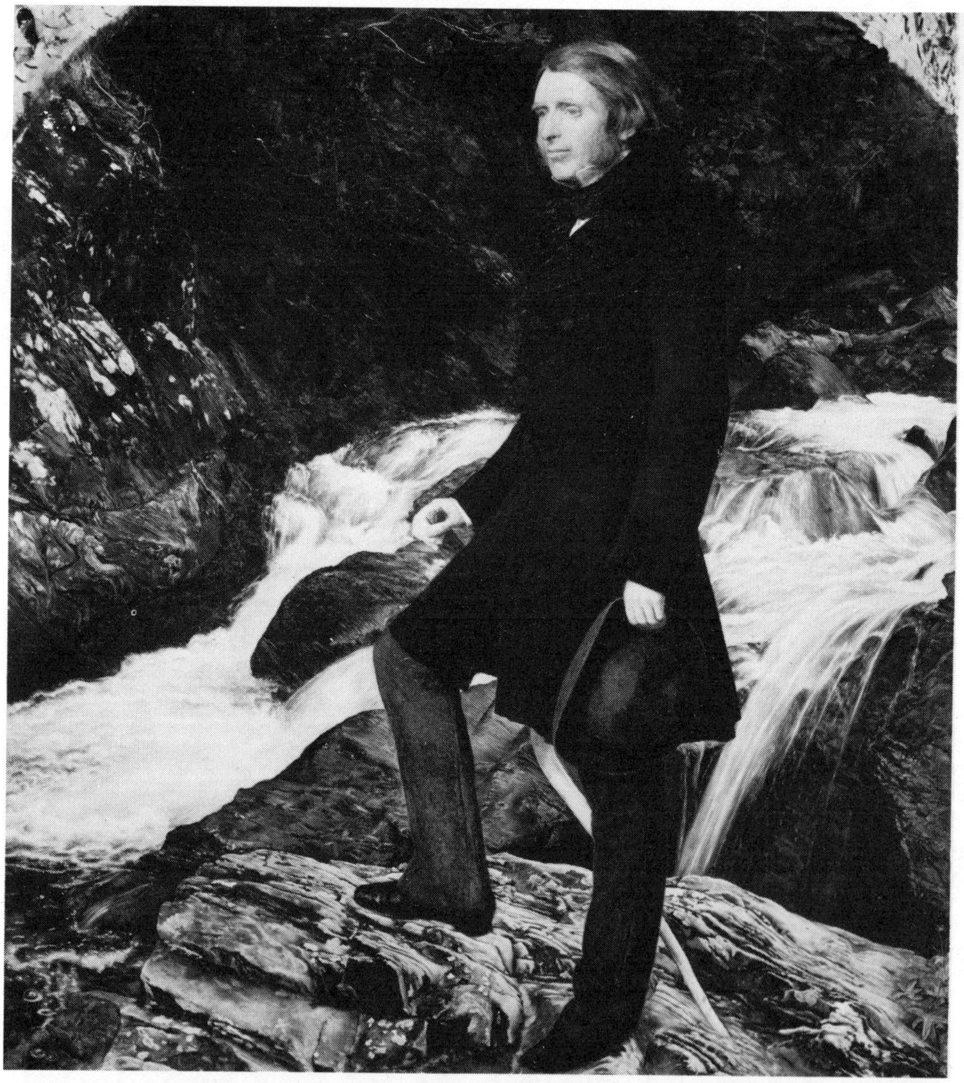

Figure 1 John Ruskin aged thirty-four, painted 1853 by (Sir) John Everett Millais at Glenfinlas, Perthshire, 'looking quietly downstream, upon a lovely piece of worn rock.' At the end of that year Ruskin's wife Effie sued successfully for annulment of the marriage, and in 1855 married Millais. (Private Collection).

been walking blindfold – this book seems to give me eyes'. Ruskin's interests then widened into architecture, especially that of mediaeval Italy. *The Seven Lamps of Architecture* (1849) and *The Stones of Venice* (1851–3) were the result.

In the late 1850s, following an unconsummated and unhappy marriage to Effie Gray (who, on its annulment, married the painter Millais), he developed his views on art and architecture into a criticism, maintained until his mind finally clouded in the 1880s, of *laissez-faire* and industrialism. His first sustained social criticism was *Unto this Last* (1862). Despite its initial unpopularity, Ruskin's reputation as prescriber for the ills of Victorian society grew, and he followed it with a series of letters and addresses on a wide range of scientific, artistic, social and political topics, published, usually under strange Latin titles, by his disciple George Allen (the founder of the firm of Allen and Unwin). In 1867, at the time of the second Reform Bill, he put forward a somewhat bizarre plan for the reconstruction of British society on the lines of a sort of feudal socialism, and attempted to follow this up by founding the Guild of St George (1871) whose ambitious aims for handcraft communities finally declined into a few small-scale projects.

Ruskin's last main public intervention was as Slade Professor of Art at Oxford (1870–4 and 1883–4), when he attempted – with much success – to preach his social gospel to the new elite of the reformed universities. But madness, which would now be diagnosed as schizophrenia, intervened, and a brief recovery (1881–3) was not sustained. He lived out the rest of his life in seclusion at Brantwood, near Coniston, living on the income of £4,000 a year brought in by his works, having given away the rest of a fortune of over £300,000. He died on 20 January 1900. Few writers of his period can have been so widely printed; the *British Museum Catalogue* lists over 550 titles of books by or about him, published between 1843 and 1950, including translations in all the main European languages.

2.2 ART

EXERCISE

In Units 22–23, *Nature, Work and Art,* Stephen Bayley devotes several pages (pp. 47–50) to Ruskin. At this stage, please re-read these. What sort of picture of Ruskin is he building?

DISCUSSION

Well, it's not terribly flattering. Stephen Bayley contends that Ruskin imposed moral criteria on pictures 'whose content was wholly aesthetic' – although he qualifies this by saying that he was 'as various and confusing a man as Turner'. He then describes Ruskin's 'moral bludgeon' as 'intimidating art in England', trying to persuade a highly-industrialized society to revert to 'an imaginary mediaeval world where the craftsman was in love with his work'.

Now there's a lot of truth in this, but I don't think it does Ruskin, or his times, full justice. For *Modern Painters* was truly an epoch-making work. As the pioneer of the re-discovery of Victorian culture, G. M. Young, wrote in *Portrait of an Age*: 'In Sydney Smith's stately compliments to the Graduate of Oxford, the eighteenth century bows itself off the stage and introduces its successor.' (Page 13.)

We have to remember that the Graduate of Oxford was not simply the wealthy son of a noted patron, but a gifted artist and a formidable writer. Read through 'Turner's Childhood' (Reader, III.3), an extract from the fifth volume of *Modern Painters* (admittedly written a lot later) and you will gain some idea of the 'punch' of his remarkable style. The book was not simply art criticism but a work of art in its own right, with its rich word-pictures of the artist's environment and subject matter. It was well fitted to catch the attention of the nouveau-riche, well-heeled art patrons (whom Jeremy Maas described in radio programme 23) eager for instruction in good taste, not having inherited it. By championing Turner, it was appropriately patriotic, and its religious attitude to art made it conform to the ethos of the day. Before 1843, remember, much fashionable painting was more like faking – producing old masters for new houses – or was rakishly pagan, like the luscious nudes of William Etty. Art had to be squared with the religious intensity of the time – this is the decade of the Oxford Movement in England the 'Disruption' in Scotland. So Ruskin's reputation in the 1840s and 1850s, when his comments on new paintings were almost holy writ, reflected an art world which was tidying itself up and elevating its moral tone.

Ruskin's social criticism was yet to come, but it arose from his 'moral seriousness'. The profundity of a painting was seen as depending on the effort required properly to examine it, which 'decoded' – as it were – the effort that a great artist – Turner, or later the Pre-Raphaelites – had given to its creation. In a way, this was not unlike the 'labour theory of value' that both Adam Smith and Karl Marx adhered to – that the value of an object was determined by the amount of work embodied in it. Hence Ruskin's later fury at James McNeill Whistler's *Falling Rocket* (1877) a painting which seems not unlike many of the late Turners Ruskin energetically defended. His language then was certainly intemperate: 'He had never expected to hear a coxcomb ask two hundred guineas for flinging a pot of paint in the public's face!' But the reason for this hostility was Whistler's view that art – or painting – should be regarded as having both technical *and moral* autonomy. 'Art for art's sake' – the ruling dogma of 'modernism' in art, was something Ruskin had no time for.

Modern Painters resulted in Ruskin being introduced to Thomas Carlyle, with profound effects on his later social philosophy. As Stuart Brown has explained in Units 28–29 *Work, Morality and Human Nature,* Carlyle preached 'the gospel of work'. Ruskin, who was a much less ferocious character, refined this by distinguishing between 'Useful Work' and 'Useless Toil'. But common to both was an apprehension about the consequences of the new 'mechanistic' industrial order. Contrast the concluding passage from *Modern Painters* reproduced below with the opening paragraph of Carlyle's 'Signs of the Times' (1829) (Reader, XVI.1):

> The fact is verily so. The great man of our England, (J. M. W. Turner), in the first half of the nineteenth century, in the strength and hope of his youth, perceives this to be the thing he has to tell us of utmost moment, connected with the spiritual world. In each city and country of past time, the master-minds had to declare the chief worship which lay at the nation's heart; to define it; adorn it; show the range and authority of it. Thus in Athens, we have the triumph of Pallas, and in Venice the Assumption of the Virgin; here, in England, is our great Spiritual fact for ever interpreted to us – the Assumption of the Dragon. No St George any more to be heard of; no more dragon-slaying possible: this child, born on St George's Day, can only make manifest the dragon, not slay him, sea-serpent as he is; whom the English Andromeda, not fearing, takes for her lord. The fairy English Queen once thought to command the waves, but it is the sea-dragon now who commands her valleys; of old the Angel of the Sea ministered to them, but now the Serpent of the Sea; where once flowed their clear springs now spread the black Cocytus[1] pool: and the fair blooming of the Hesperid[2] meadows fades into ashes beneath the Nereid's[3] Guard.
>
> Yes, Albert of Nuremberg;[4] the time has at last come. Another nation has arised in the strength of its Black anger; and another hand has portrayed the spirit of its toil. Crowned with fire, and with the wings of the bat. (*Modern Painters,* Vol. V, Part IX, ch. X, page 25.)

[1]Cocytus: from Greek mythology, a river in Hades.

[2]Hesperid: from the Hesperides, in Greek mythology, 'the fortunate isles'.

[3]Nereid: from Greek mythology, sea-nymph.

[4]Albert of Nuremberg: Albrecht Dürer (1471–1528), German painter and his engraving 'The Four Horsemen of the Apocalypse'.

2.3 ARCHITECTURE

The successive volumes of *Modern Painters* saw Ruskin's art criticism widen into social criticism. Some would say that, as an art critic, he scarcely developed. For instance, he was still writing as the Impressionists painted in Paris, but he seems to have been oblivious of their existence. On the other hand others would argue, with Ruskin himself, that if one had moral expectations of art, the logical thing to do was to concentrate on 'the greater arts', the design of the buildings that housed people's lives, work and worship. *The Seven Lamps of Architecture* – Truth, Beauty, Power, Sacrifice, Obedience, Labour, Memory (although Ruskin said he could add several more if he wanted to) – became the textbook for a generation of architects. Its lessons were enforced by the practical examples of *The Stones of Venice*. This was an even tighter equation of aesthetics with ethics. Its opening sentences announced bluntly that Britain's economic success did not entitle her to moral supremacy:

> Since first the dominion of men was asserted over the ocean, three thrones, of mark beyond all others, have been set upon its sands: the thrones of Tyre, Venice and England. Of the First of these great powers only the memory remains; of the Second, the ruins; the Third, which inherits their greatness, if it forget their example, may be led through prouder eminence to less pitied destruction. (*The Stones of Venice* Vol. I, 1851.)

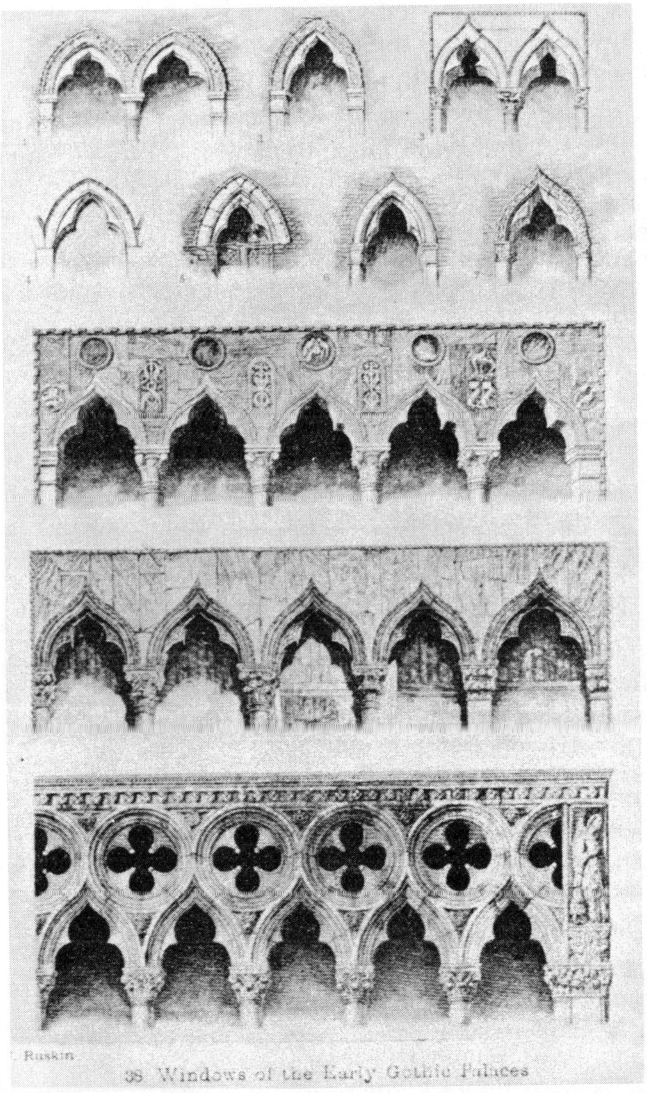

Figure 2 Windows of the Early Gothic Palaces, Drawing by John Ruskin. (Photo from J. Ruskin (1906) The Stones of Venice, *George Allen, Vol II, opposite page 257.)*

Again, external factors (about which Ruskin must have had mixed feelings) ensured that both books would make a significant impact. Italy was being opened up to tourists. The railway reached Venice in 1846, and in the 1850s Cook's tourist parties were becoming commonplace in its hotels. At the same time, in Britain, the movement in architectural taste towards electicism, or variety of styles, and in particular away from classicism, ensured that his advocacy of Venetian gothic would be well received, while the Protestant impulse in Ruskin which led him to prefer the austere gothic of the earlier church to the elaborate classicism of the Renaissance, made Venice more attractive to the English than Rome. Less than a century earlier, a not unrepresentative traveller, Edward Gibbon, had written of the Rialto and St Mark's Square:

> . . . old and in general, ill-built houses, ruined pictures, and stinking ditches, dignified with the pompous denomination of canals, a fine bridge spoilt by two rows of houses on it, and a large square decorated with the worst architecture I ever saw. (Letter to his stepmother, 22 April 1765, quoted in E. T. Cook, *The Life of Ruskin* Vol. 1, page 302.)

After *The Stones of Venice* this changed dramatically, 'We do not remember' said a writer in the *North British Review* in May 1854 'anything in the history of art in England at all corresponding in suddenness and extent to the effect which the works of Mr Ruskin have already exercised on the popular taste directly, and through popular taste on the taste and theories of artists themselves.' (Quoted in Cook, *The Life of Ruskin,* page 305.)

In so far as this impact merely influenced the repertoire of architectural styles, however, Ruskin lived to regret it. Soon he was lamenting the growth of 'Venetian' warehouses, churches and pubs, and by the mid-1860s could write:

> The architecture we endeavoured to introduce is inconsistent alike with the reckless luxury, the deforming mechanism, and the squalid misery of modern cities; among the formative fashions of the day, aided, especially in England, by ecclesiastical sentiment, it indeed obtained notoriety; and sometimes behind an engine-furnace, or a railroad bank, you may detect the pathetic discord of its momentary grace, and, with toil, decipher its floral carvings choked with soot. I felt answerable to the schools I loved, only for their injury. ('The Mystery of Life and Its Arts' in *Sesame and Lilies,* 1866.)

EXERCISE

Read through the extract 'Rochdale and Pisa' (Reader, IX.2). What was Ruskin's main complaint about the manufacturing towns of Victorian England?

SPECIMEN ANSWER

Ruskin argues that the conditions for great art, of the standard of Pisa, cannot exist in the squalor of places like Rochdale, because the creation of wealth – regardless of the consequences – is given more predominance than the quality of life of the mass of the people.

EXERCISE

From what you've read about Ruskin and Venice in this section, what message did he use the parallel between Pisa, or Venice, and England to convey? Was this simply an argument for a return to a mediaeval past?

SPECIMEN ANSWER

The wealth of the great mediaeval commercial city was spent in a way that added to the culture of the whole world. Nineteenth-century England – of equivalent prestige in its time – seemed simply to be squandering resources and leaving little of value. Ruskin specifically rejects mediaevalism, arguing that where there is exploitation, in whatever age, social collapse will follow.

DISCUSSION

Venice, to the Victorians was a symbol both of past and future. It was the pre-eminent example of commercial civilization whose style the British urban middle class attempted to emulate; it also represented the dignified remains of an industrial state after its commercial supremacy had departed. This was the burden of Ruskin's 'Sermon in Stones': not a new style of decorative architecture, but a demand for urban reconstruction and a responsible urban elite. At this level, Ruskin influenced many of the leaders of the public health movement, like Sir John Simon (the Chief Medical Officer to the Privy Council after 1855) and Octavia Hill (whose efforts for improved working-class dwellings and charity organization laid, albeit in a paternalist manner, the basis of modern social casework).

But his influence went further. Like W. E. Forster (Units 24–25, *The Experience of Industrialization*, Section 14) he responded to Carlyle's criticism of the supremacy of commercial over social goals. The impact of industrial organization in general and machinery in particular, coupled with the European revolutions of 1848, increased awareness among the elite of the danger of estrangement between classes. Practically, this led to his involvement after 1854 in the Working Men's College, an enterprise of the Christian Socialists, theoretically it led to the section of *The Stones of Venice* entitled 'The Nature of Gothic', where he extended Carlyle's vivid perception of the mechanization of society to condemn the consequences of the division of labour. It seemed to him that unless men could profit from, enjoy and be secure in their work their discontent could reach explosive dimensions.

3 RUSKIN ON ECONOMICS

The trades unionists and socialists who provided the market for the thousands of cheap editions of Ruskin's writings sold before 1914 were influenced by Ruskin's economics more than by his art-criticism, although the two were closely linked, both in Ruskin's own writings and in his influence on the socialist William Morris. As the latter wrote in his preface to the Kelmscott Press edition of 'The Nature of Gothic':

> John Ruskin, the teacher of morals and politics, has done serious and solid work toward the new-birth of society, without which genuine art, the expression of man's pleasure in his handiwork, must inevitably cease altogether, and with it the hopes of the happiness of mankind. (Quoted in James Ramsay Macdonald, 'William Morris', in *Prophets of the Century*, page 268.)

His economic influence was, however, not limited to socialists. John Atkinson Hobson (1858–1940), one of the most influential economic thinkers of the twentieth century, wrote in his autobiography:

> From him I drew the basic thought for my subsequent economic writings, viz. the necessity of going behind the current monetary estimates of wealth, cost and utility to reach the body of human benefits and satisfactions which give them a real meaning. (Hobson, *Confessions of An Economic Heretic*, page 42.)

EXERCISE

How did Ruskin's economic thought differ from the tradition against which it reacted? and how did it differ from the 'scientific socialism' of Marx and Engels? To grasp what the essentials of these doctrines were, go back and re-read Unit 21, *Key Concepts*, pp. 11–16 and Units 24–25, *The Experience of Industrialization*, pp. 73–4.

DISCUSSION

From this, you will see that 'classical' economists who advocated industrialization, generalizing rather too easily from *The Wealth of Nations*, thought that the 'invisible hand' of market economics would secure economic growth and social development without anyone having to consult anything more than his own self-interest. Nations were similar; it was rational for them to live at peace with one another and trade together, each specializing in the economic activity it was best suited to. Out of the links built up by such international trade would come international understanding, as it would be in no-one's interest for one nation to advance its own concerns through war. Thus, in Goldwin Smith's words, 'one heart as well as one harvest for the world' would be the outcome of industrialization.

Overall, Karl Marx's view wasn't dissimilar: he saw the struggle as one within states rather than as one between states. The capitalists would maintain peace because it suited them. Wars between nations were old-fashioned: the war the workers would have to prepare for was the civil war which would end capitalism.

In this way both capitalism and 'scientific' socialism were rational *and* utopian. Both were predicated on the idea that the laws of economics were 'natural' – capable of scientific prediction – and both entailed an underestimation of the irrational in man's nature.

But, even in Adam Smith's day these 'natural laws' of economics could conflict with the 'natural tendency' of groups of businessmen to conspire against the public interest by rigging the market in their own favour. (Remember Units 24–25, *The Experience of Industrialization*, Section 5.) Government intervention was inevitable, to keep competition fair, to prevent 'natural monopolies' – land, rivers, some forms of transport – being exploited by privileged groups, and later to protect infant and strategically-important industries.

So, even at a time when the supremacy of *laissez-faire* economics was accepted throughout Europe, here are two major constraints, caused by the conflict of the 'natural' qualities of men: their unequal economic power and their social organization into nation-states. It was in this context that Ruskin's arguments took effect.

EXERCISE

At this stage I'd like you to read the extract from John Ruskin's 'The Veins of Wealth' (1862) (Reader, XVII.8), beginning at 'I would not contend . . .' on page 263 and ending at '. . . the resources of the body politic' on page 265. The book this extract is taken from, *Unto this Last*, was published as a series of articles in the *Cornhill Magazine* in 1860 when it caused a furore among the magazine's middle-class readership so great that the articles had to be discontinued. Why do you think this was? How would you describe Ruskin's picture of his two economies? What is his message, for men and for states?

DISCUSSION

I'm not going to give a specimen answer but I'll go through the passage with you and suggest possible interpretations.

By 'mercantile' economy Ruskin obviously means the ruling *laissez-faire* attitude to resources, where everything is given a price and exploited for it. In particular he argues that the wealth of the British middle class is secured at the expense of others, and by the power over labour which it uses its wealth to exert. How would we like to be told in 1862 that our own own modest wealth, our villa in Wimbledon, was the result of 'establishing the maximum inequality in our favour'?

If 'exploitation' is the keynote of his description of 'mercantile economy', 'conservation' is surely the keynote of his 'political economy'. This means the consideration of long-term values which can't directly be measured in economic terms. 'The housewife who takes care of her furniture in the parlour, and guards against all waste in her kitchen; and the singer who rightly disciplines, and never overstrains her voice': both are taking natural care of their resources, where 'mercenary' economics might suggest that the housewife ought to buy new rather than mend, or the singer ought to sing herself out for the biggest possible return in the shortest possible time.

Ruskin argues, surely, that to treat this 'natural' economy by the laws of 'mercenary' economy is self-evidently daft. But this is the natural effect of great differences of wealth in society, and of the exploitation of resources, human and natural, which does not allow for 'well-rounded' development, both of individuals and of states.

Ruskin's attitudes could be applied to the relations between states. Was the wealth of Britain secured by the poverty of the countries whose native industries she destroyed by flooding their markets with cheap imports? Nations, like people, could have their personalities ruined by over-specialization and exploitation.

Ruskin was, in fact, Victorian enough to be an enthusiastic imperialist, though for moral reasons rather than economic ones, but two of his most enthusiastic disciples, J. A. Hobson and the Indian leader Mohandas Gandhi (1868–1948) were to turn elements of his insights into powerful political weapons against Western imperialism.

In his book *Imperialism* (1900) Hobson argued in an essentially Ruskinian fashion that the continuing exploitation of the British working class by capitalism led to 'under-consumption' at home. This meant that the domestic market for goods and investment was always limited and capital had to migrate abroad, to the new imperial territories, to get a sufficiently large return. Subsequent historical evidence has knocked holes in Hobson's thesis – capital had to be forced into the Empire by governments; it rarely migrated there of its own accord – but it was pirated by Lenin (1870–1924), leader of the Bolshevik or majority wing of the Russian Social Democrats, to argue in *Imperialism; The Highest Stage of Capitalism* (1916) that the advanced capitalist powers were engaging in a scramble for territory which was bound both to cause conflict and to suck the whole world – developed and undeveloped – into a global crisis of capitalism. This conflict would give the Bolsheviks their chance, even in backward, peasant-dominated Russia.

With Gandhi we return to Ruskin's argument against the machine: that mass-production industry both degrades and enslaves. We noticed in Units 24–25, *The Experience of Industrialization*, Section 2 how the Lancashire cotton industry began by imitating Indian cottons. Soon it had not only destroyed their export market in Britain, but its production costs were so cheap that it could replace them in India as well, destroying the hand-work industries of the Indian villages. In this way India suffered not only economic enslavement, but the destruction by British mass-production techniques of industries vital to her cohesion as a community. Against this Gandhi, who had been introduced to Ruskin's writings via *Unto this Last* in 1904, created in the symbol of the spinning-wheel something which stood both for the self-sufficiency of village India and for opposition to British rule. Here again, the ideal of development was taken as the completeness of the person or of the nation, and the superiority of both to the 'mercantile economy' of imperialism.

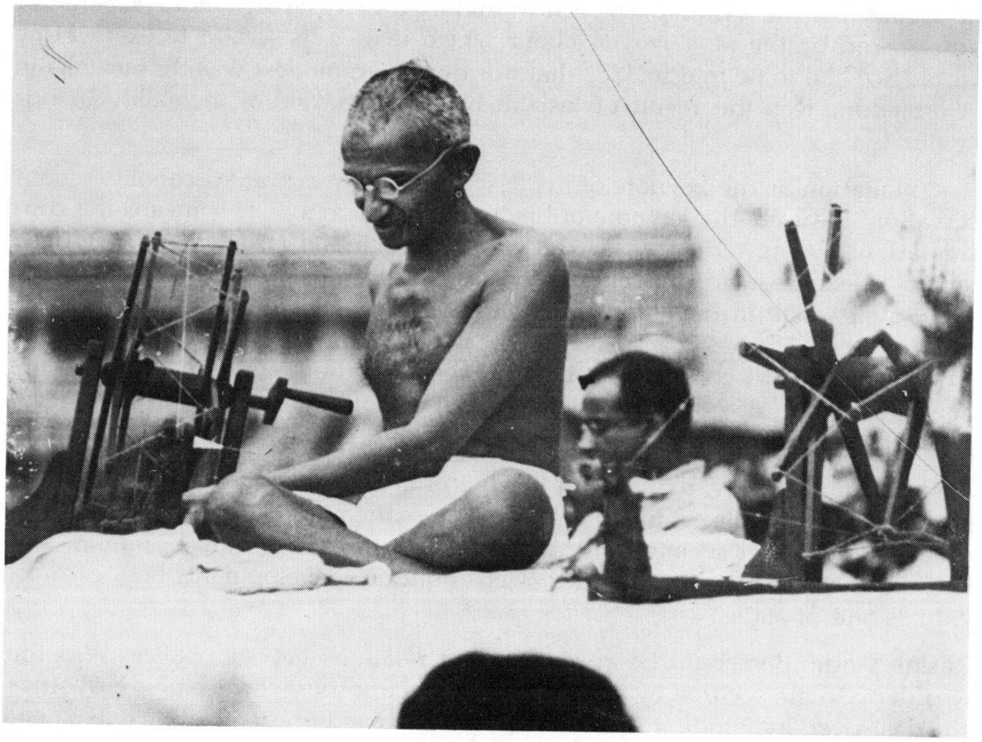

Figure 3 Gandhi spinning at a 'charka' demonstration in Mirzapore Park, Calcutta in 1925 (Radio Times Hulton Picture Library).

In Britain after the Second World War, reformulations of 'classical' economics, like that of J. M. Keynes (1883–1946), designed to overcome unemployment in developed countries, specifically rejected any moral purpose beyond that of promoting growth and employment. Keynes was a noted patron of the arts, and effective founder of the Arts Council, but culture was to him essentially 'high culture' to be bought by the dividends on economic growth of virtually any sort (including arms expenditure and 'conspicuous consumption'). But the question of the relationship between economics and ethics has reasserted its importance today, with the depletion of resources in 'developed' countries, and the failure of industrialization – capitalist or communist – to bring either prosperity or freedom to the mass of 'third world' citizens, while in the writing of contemporary economists like E. F. Schumacher and E. J. Mishan, who are deeply critical of the panacea of economic growth, many of Ruskin's concerns have reemerged.

4 RUSKIN, NATURE AND ECOLOGY

In radio programme 25 I looked at the way in which, during the industrial expansion of Britain, natural resources became totally subject to economic exploitation by man. Dependence on wind and water for power gave way to dependence on fossil fuel, and by the 1860s the prospect of an energy shortage was being entertained. In other words an industrial order dependent, to a certain degree, on natural chance had now yielded to one which exploited natural resources. With the extension of scientific knowledge about the natural world – geology, botany and, most significant of all, biology – nature came, purely and simply, to be evaluated as a resource. Land was there to be cultivated, stone to be quarried; animals to be bred, shorn, slaughtered. The great extension of European culture during the Victorian period was directly connected with this. 'Rushes' for gold or diamonds opened up California, Australia and New Zealand from the 1840s on, to be succeeded by the exploitation of natural substances like rubber in Malaya, asphalte in Trinidad and phosphates in South America, and, for that matter, oil after 1908, when the Anglo-Persian Oil Company discovered its first 'gusher' at Masjid-i-Sulaiman in South Iran.

Here is Ruskin's reaction to this sort of development: part of an address to the Bradford Chamber of Commerce in 1859.

> The extent of our operations at present is more or less limited by the extent of coal and ironstone, but we have not yet learned to make proper use of our clay. Over the greater part of England, south of the manufacturing districts, there are magnificent beds of various kinds of useful clay; and I believe that it would not be difficult to point out modes of employing it which might enable us to turn nearly the whole of the south of England into a brickfield, as we have already turned nearly the whole of the north into a coal-pit. I say 'nearly' the whole, because, as you are doubtless aware, there are considerable districts in the south composed of chalk, renowned up to the present time for their downs and mutton. But, I think, by examining carefully into the conceivable uses of chalk, we might discover a quite feasible probability of turning all the chalk districts into a limekiln, as we turn the clay districts into a brickfield. There would then remain nothing but the mountain districts to be dealt with; but, as we have not yet ascertained all the uses of clay and chalk, still less have we ascertained those of stone; and I think, by draining the useless inlets of the Cumberland, Welsh, and Scotch lakes, and turning them, with their rivers, into navigable reservoirs and canals, there would be no difficulty in working the whole of our mountain districts as a gigantic quarry of slate and granite, from which all the rest of the world might be supplied with roofing and building stone.

EXERCISE

What point is Ruskin trying to make about the relation between economics and the natural world?

DISCUSSION

Surely, that if your economics are 'mercantile', concerned only with exploitation for cash profit, you can only judge the natural world as a resource, not as something to be enjoyed for itself.

This picture was surrealistic – almost a word-rendering of one of John Martin's wilder creations – but not all that far from actuality, given the relentless expansion of the towns and the exploitation for industrial reasons of even the most remote areas of England like the Lake District and the High Peak. The 1860s was, in fact, the first time that the impact of industrialization was seen as permanently unbalancing the natural world.

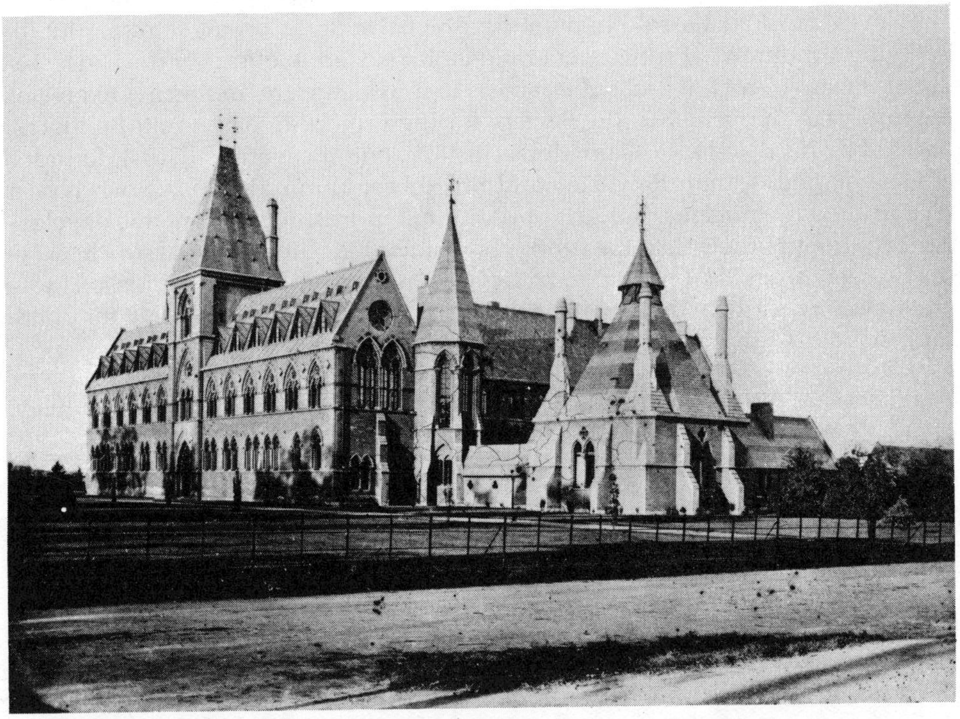

Figure 4 The University Museum in the Parks, Oxford. Ruskin played a major part in furthering this project for the organization of science teaching at Oxford. It was housed in this Gothic building, designed by Deane and Woodward of Dublin, and built 1855–60. Ruskin called it 'literally the first building raised in England since the fifteenth century, which has fearlessly put to new trial this old faith in nature, and in the genius of the unassisted workman'. But his plans to allow the workmen to use their initiative in decorating it were frustrated by the authorities, and it never fulfilled his expectations. (Photo from The National Monuments Record, London.)

Ruskin was not a sentimentalist about nature; he was a gifted botanist and geologist, and the friend of many leading scientists. As much, say, as the positivist Auguste Comte, he believed that one could derive laws for human conduct from observation of the natural sciences. He did not believe that the laws of market economics were so derived. You can see this contrast in the quotations from *Modern Painters*:

> In substance which we call 'inanimate', as of clouds, or stones, their atoms may cohere to each other, or consist with each other, but they do not help each other. The removal of one part does not injure the rest.
>
> But in a plant, the taking away of any one part does injure the rest. Hurt or remove any portion of the sap, bark, or pith, the rest is injured. If any part enters into a state in which it no more assists the rest, and has thus become 'helpless', we call it also 'dead'.
>
> The power which causes the several portions of the plant to help each other, we call life. Much more is this so in an animal. We may take away the branch of a tree without much harm to it; but not the animal's limb. Thus, intensity of life is also intensity of helpfulness – completeness of depending of each part on all the rest. The ceasing of this help is what we call corruption; and in proportion to the perfectness of the help, is the dreadfulness of the loss. The more intense the life has been, the more terrible is its corruption.
>
> [Later, concluding a description of how a gem is formed:]
>
> And, for the ounce of slime which we had by political economy of competition, we have by political economy of cooperation, a sapphire, an opal, and a diamond, set in the midst of a star of snow. (*Modern Painters*, Vol. V, 1860, Part VIII, ch. 1, pp. 4, 8–9.)

This conviction was summed up in his famous phrase: 'Competition and Anarchy are Laws of Death; Government and Cooperation are Laws of Life', and led directly to his 'organic' view of society and to the desire that economic development should not be allowed to prejudice the balance, or 'ecology', of nature, or the living conditions of future generations. It also led to efforts at the conservation of the environment and public access to it, which were, indirectly, to give us two important movements: the Society for the Protection of Ancient Buildings, founded by his disciple William Morris in 1877, and the National Trust, founded by Octavia Hill, Canon Rawnsley and Sir Robert Hunter in 1895. Such bodies have formed the nucleus of much opposition to unrestricted economic development, although their activities today still raise questions similar to those of Ruskin's own day. Is opposition to development simply the reaction of those who have already benefited by it, as the Keynesian economist and Labour politician, the late Anthony Crosland, put it?

> They are affluent and fundamentally, though of course not consciously, they want to kick the ladder down behind them. They are highly selective in their concern, being militant mainly about threats to rural peace and wild-life and well-loved beauty-spots; they are little concerned with the far more desperate problem of the urban environment in which 80 per cent of our fellow citizens live. (*A Social Democratic Britain*, page 5.)

5 RUSKIN AS A VICTORIAN SAGE: INSIGHTS AND LIMITATIONS

'INSIGHTS' VERSUS 'SYSTEMS'

> I have not yet read Ruskin's new book (*Time and Tide*): the title is perhaps vulgar: Ruskin is full of follies but I get more and more sympathetic with the 'true men' as against the Sophistik . . . Philistine, Doctrinaire, Utilitarian, Positive, and on the whole Negative (as Carlyle would put it) side, and prefer to err with Plato. (Hopkins to A. W. M. Baillie, 12 February, 1868, quoted in *Gerard Manley Hopkins: Poems and Prose,* page 166.)

Thus the young Gerard Manley Hopkins wrote in 1868. If you read his poem 'Binsey Poplars' (Reader, XXV.1) you will grasp an awareness of man's insensitivity to the balance of the natural world, which plainly owes something to Ruskin. Hopkins himself used to talk of the 'inscape' of his poems and prose writings – their attempt to perceive the natural world as something with a life of its own 'the outward reflection of the inner nature of the thing', and not simply an 'external scene'. Lord Clark has noted that this echoes Ruskin's aesthetics: his defence of Turner against those who criticized his late paintings for their obscurity: 'Light is proportioned to the power of the eye; feeling to the depth of the soul.'

If we are to understand the importance of the sages, and the contents list of a fairly typical book *Prophets of the Century,* published in 1898, gives a useful core – Wordsworth, Shelley, Carlyle, Emerson, Tennyson, George Eliot, Ruskin, Whitman, Morris, Tolstoy and Ibsen – we have to understand the impact of a phrase like 'the depth of the soul'. 'The Philistine, Doctrinaire, Utilitarian, Positive' side dismissed this idea of the human soul being distinct and unique. If, after David Hartley, Benthamites believed the mind to be made up of sense-impressions (Units 28–29, *Work, Morality and Human Nature,* Section 2.2), then the idea of an individual 'soul' was impossible. Robert Owen (1771–1858) the factory owner whose social experiments at New Lanark (1805–19) prefigured Soviet social planning as well as capitalist 'scientific management', placed particular stress on education for this reason and the 'Halls of Science' founded by his followers tended to be dominated by friezes with the text: 'The Character of Man is formed for and not by him'.

Here you have an important paradox within industrial society. Industrialization had been based on competitive individualism, yet 'classical' economics and sociology taught that the behaviour of individuals varied in accordance with a limited number of stimuli, and regarded it as being quite predictable. Far from freeing men, *laissez-faire* seemed to trap them in a new and rigid environment. Men were also thought of as being basically equal in ability, but the richness of life available to the well-off meant that they were at a permanent advantage, and could eventually come to regard those at the bottom of the heap as a subhuman species. These 'survival of the fittest' inclinations provide one reason for the importance of evolutionary ideas and 'social-Darwinism' to the Victorian middle class.

The Victorian sages revolted against the tyranny of rigid systems of thought, like the 'machinery' satirized by Carlyle in 'Signs of the Times'. Their motives were usually centred on a belief in the individual's character – not simply his mind – which could overcome his environment. As Carlyle wrote in 1839, contrasting the two social extremes of contemporary Britain, the impoverished Irishman and the aristocrat:

> The Sanspotato is of the selfsame stuff as the superfinest Lord Lieutenant. Not an individual Sanspotato but had a life given him out of Heaven with Eternities depending on it; for once and no second time. With Immensities in him, over him and around him; with feelings which a Shakespeare's speech would not utter; with desires as illimitable as the Autocrat's of all the Russias. (Carlyle, *Chartism*.)

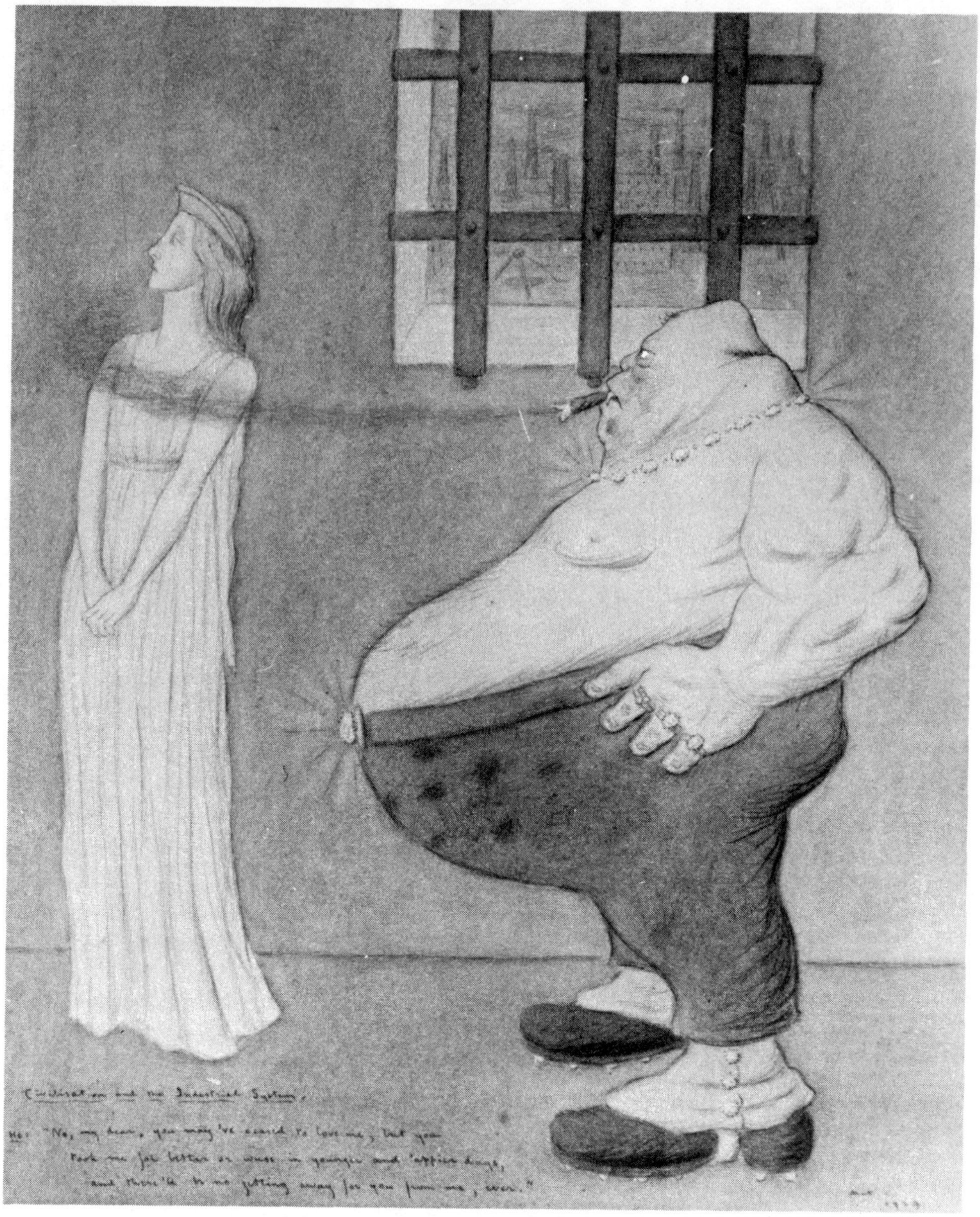

Figure 5 Max Beerbohm, Civilisation and the Industrialisation System, *drawing, 1929. The caption reads 'He: "No, my dear, you may've ceased to love me; but you took me for better or wuss in younger and 'appier days, and there'll be no getting away for you from me, ever." ' (L. J. Cadbury)*

This 'common humanity', what Dostoevsky called 'the spark of God in every man', implied an attitude to man which was essentially religious rather than rational, even though it coincided with a period in which religious belief was declining. And a 'religious' view of humanity, like a romantic one, exalted emotion, imagination and feeling over calculation and system-building.

Formal religion was losing its grip on the mass of the population, as well as on the intellectuals. (See Units 24–25, *The Experience of Industrialization,* Section 11.) By the mid-1860s, this was becoming glaringly apparent, following the Census of 1851 and the violent clashes between churchmen and scholars in 1860 over the rationalistic *Essays and Reviews* and Darwin's *Origin of Species* (both published in 1859). In the 1830s Providence was still thought to play some part in human affairs. Parliament in 1832 declared a national day of prayer which it hoped would end the cholera epidemic; Providence still plays a critical role in several sections of *Jane Eyre*. But by the 1860s and 1870s the cultural vocabulary was much more secular, although few people would have assented wholeheartedly to the materialism of the scientists.

It was into this religious perplexity that various 'secular gospels', expressed with religious symbolism and language, came. Carlyle was probably the pioneer. Stuart Brown has mentioned Samuel Smiles and the 'Gospel of Work' (Unit 28–29 Section 4.4), and there were also the Positivists with their 'religion of humanity'. In these ways 'non-doctrinaire' religion – and social criticism – was tied to Victorian liberalism and individualism as well as to orthodox Christianity. It urged people to exert their own personalities against a system, nominally libertarian, which threatened to grind them into conformity, and could range from the 'religious' approach to secular individualism of John Stuart Mill, the 'saint of rationalism' in *On Liberty* (1859) to the 'liberal Catholicism' of John Henry, Cardinal Newman, which was to claim a convert in Gerard Manley Hopkins. It was this society which readily appreciated Ruskin's 'Sermons in Stones'.

Yet despite secularization, the future did not lie with the calculators and system-builders, for what they failed to do was to explore the subconscious mind. But by the time of the outbreak of the First World War, they had, at least on the continent, been dethroned. Under the influence of, among others, the sociologists Emile Durkheim and Max Weber, the psychologists Sigmund Freud and Carl Gustav Jung, and the novelists Thomas Mann and Marcel Proust, the human personality and the relations between man and society were seen as something complex, and the part of them that was subject to rationality was merely the tip of the iceberg. As the American intellectual historian Stuart Hughes wrote in *Consciousness and Society* (1958):

> Men were masters of their fate, they argued, only for limited periods and in strictly limited segments of their activity. The eighteenth- or early nineteenth-century image of man as a self-consciously rational being freely selecting among properly weighed alternatives they dismissed as an antiquated illusion. (Page 4.)

This generation attempted to explore both the mechanisms within the social arrangements and the individual subconscious which integrated the individual with society, and what happened when this integration failed. On the one hand this involved examining religion, the family, and leadership; on the other social violence, madness and suicide.

This re-orientation of social thought was more significant on the continent than in Britain but Ruskin, who was widely read on the continent, was one of the thinkers who contributed to it, both directly through his writings and indirectly through his own tragic personal history. For Marcel Proust, in particular, Ruskin, as a 'Spirit of Intercession', provided both through his writings on art and though his self-analysis in *Praeterita*, 'an understanding of the Middle Ages, a sense of history, and the feeling of a sort of natural sympathy for all things that have grown dim with age, and an awareness of their continuing presence'. (Quoted in Maurois, *The Quest for Proust*, page 113.) In extending the bounds of the European novel to embrace time, consciousness and memory Ruskin therefore played a critical if catalytic role. Moreover, in the nature of his mental collapse, his career could raise the sort of problem entertained later by the psychologists: what determined madness? Repressed sexuality, as Freud argued, or the insanity within social organization itself?

6 RUSKIN TODAY

Apart from historians and art historians, few people today read many of the Victorian sages, let alone Ruskin. Is this neglect of what he actually wrote justified? If you find a copy, read Ruskin's description of the approach to Venice from the beginning of Volume II of *The Stones of Venice.* I think that you'll find that his 'purple passages' involve an expertise in using words, a restraint and sense of proportion that give them a calculated as well as an emotional impact comparable with romantic masterpieces like say, Bruckner's symphonies, or Turner's paintings.

Nowadays we need not describe scenes verbally that we can transmit by photographic image, so that this sort of craftsmanship is at a discount: more important as an historical phenomenon than as something of contemporary interest. Much of Ruskin's achievement has likewise been eroded by historical change. The decline in religious belief has meant that arguments about squaring religion and scientific progress no longer exert the fascination they once did; women have long ago rejected the life of contented domesticity that was all Ruskin offered them.

But his ideas still remain important, in two main aspects. Firstly, their influence during the nineteenth century affected a wide range of social and political movements. This influence may have been like that of a chemical catalyst, which causes a reaction to take place while not surviving as part of the new substance, but it was essential. Secondly, they were in themselves fundamental criticisms of the new industrial order, which subsequent critics tend to return to again and again because of the power and force with which they are expressed. Even if Ruskin as a whole is scarcely read, phrases like 'You must either make a tool of the creature, of a man of him', or 'it is not . . . the labour that is divided, but the men', or 'there is no wealth but life', and the ideas behind them, still stud our discussions of contemporary industrial and environmental problems.

But I don't want to end on a dogmatic note. Ruskin contributed to a range of institutions and a stock of ideas, often contradictory, which are still vital today, so I want you to look for them in the arguments contained in three 'recent' extracts, from politics, political journalism and poetry:

1 From *Labour Weekly,* reporting the Labour Party conference, 7 October 1977

> CHALLENGE TO ATOMIC POWER AVERTED
>
> Opponents of nuclear energy agreed to remit their motion on Tuesday rather than face what looked like being a massive defeat on the Windscale reprocessing plant.
>
> Their motion called for a halt on all nuclear developments, including the £600 million scheme to expand Windscale, which will lead to the development of fast breeder reactors.
>
> It was strongly opposed by three major trade union figures: Joe Gormley, Frank Chapple, and AUEW executive member Gavin Laird, who attacked the 'hysterical and inaccurate propaganda' of the anti-nuclear lobby.
>
> Energy Secretary Tony Benn, who replied for the Executive, said it would be 'wrong to call a halt now to the development of nuclear energy'.
>
> 'The world will have to rely on a major nuclear component to prevent economic growth from grinding to a halt at the start of the next century.'
>
> Tim Heffernan, moving the resolution for Leeds West, said the anti-nuclear lobby were not Luddites, nor were they middle-class dreamers with windmills or watermills in their back gardens.
>
> 'We're in favour of the development of science and technology, even nuclear technology, but in a rational and planned way' he said.

But these speakers were outweighed by the three trade union leaders starting with Joe Gormley, who called on Conference to be 'progressive' and not to pass resolutions that would 'send us back to the jungle'.

Frank Chapple, of the EETPU, said the dangers of nuclear energy were outweighed by the 'peril to the world if sources of energy run out'. Deaths from cold, hunger and poverty would be far greater.

Gavin Laird brought some heat into the debate when he attacked the 'publicity seekers who find their way to the Windscale inquiry but who have no interest in the nuclear industry'.

He maintained bluntly that 'there is no practical alternative to the expansion of nuclear energy, whether you like it or not'.

2 George Orwell, from 'Rudyard Kipling', 1943[1]

But because Kipling identifies himself with the official class, he does possess one thing which 'enlightened' people seldom or never possess, and that is a sense of responsibility. The middle-class Left hate him for this quite as much as for his cruelty and vulgarity. All left-wing parties in the highly industrialised countries are at bottom a sham, because they make it their business to fight against something which they do not really wish to destroy. They have internationalist aims, and at the same time they struggle to keep up a standard of life with which those aims are incompatible. We all live by robbing Asiatic coolies, and those of us who are 'enlightened' all maintain that those coolies ought to be set free; but our standard of living, and hence our 'enlightenment', demands that the robbery shall continue. A humanitarian is always a hypocrite, and Kipling's understanding of this is perhaps the central secret of his power to create telling phrases. It would be difficult to hit off the one-eyed pacifism of the English in fewer words than in the phrase, 'making mock of uniforms that guard you while you sleep'. It is true that Kipling does not understand the economic aspect of the relationship between the highbrow and the blimp. He does not see that the map is painted red chiefly in order that the coolie may be exploited. Instead of the coolie he sees the Indian Civil Servant; but even on that plane his grasp of function, of who protects whom, is very sound. He sees clearly that men can only be highly civilised while other men, inevitably less civilised, are there to guard and feed them.

3 Philip Larkin, 'Going, Going'[2]

Going, Going

I thought it would last my time –
The sense that, beyond the town,
There would always be fields and farms,
Where the village louts could climb
Such trees as were not cut down;
I knew there'd be false alarms

In the papers about old streets
And split-level shopping, but some
Have always been left so far;
And when the old parts retreat
As the bleak high-risers come
We can always escape in the car.

Things are tougher than we are, just
As earth will always respond
However we mess it about;
Chuck filth in the sea, if you must:
The tides will be clean beyond.
– But what do I feel now? Doubt?

[1]Reprinted in *Critical Essays*, 1954, Secker and Warburg, pp. 115–16.

[2]From *High Windows*, 1974, Faber, pp. 21–2.

Or age, simply? The crowd
Is young in the M1 café;
Their kids are screaming for more –
More houses, more parking allowed,
More caravan sites, more pay.
On the Business Page, a score

Of spectacled grins approve
Some takeover bid that entails
Five per cent profit (and ten
Per cent more in the estuaries): move
Your works to the unspoilt dales
(Grey area grants)! And when

You try to get near the sea
In summer . . .
It seems, just now,
To be happening so very fast;
Despite all the land left free
For the first time I feel somehow
That it isn't going to last,

That before I snuff it, the whole
Boiling will be bricked in
Except for the tourist parts –
First slum of Europe: a role
It won't be so hard to win,
With a cast of crooks and tarts.

And that will be England gone,
The shadows, the meadows, the lanes,
The guildhalls, the carved choirs.
There'll be books; it will linger on
In galleries; but all that remains
For us will be concrete and tyres.

Most things are never meant.
This won't be, most likely: but greeds
And garbage are too thick-strewn
To be swept up now, or invent
Excuses that make them all needs.
I just think it will happen, soon.

PART 2 INDUSTRIALIZATION AND MODERN ART IN ENGLAND

Although, as was noted in Unit 21, *Key Concepts,* the effects of industrialization and of technological development had already by 1850 been such as to transform many of those conditions of individual human life and of general human society which had been stable for eighteen centuries, many of the progressive artists and critics in the early twentieth century were preoccupied by the idea of a 'break with the past', which they saw themselves as in process of making.

The few years before the outbreak of the First World War can be seen as a kind of watershed in English culture, when many of the prevailing issues which have been discussed in the preceding units were recapitulated and transformed in the context of the twentieth century.

During this period two competing interpretations of the history of recent art prevailed. Of course few artists or writers will fit neatly and exactly into either of the categories I am about to suggest. The purpose of the distinction I'm making is to characterize an important area of controversy relevant to the early history of modern art, and to relate the issues involved to themes discussed in earlier units. I hope thus to suggest ways in which you may see continuity in the study of art during the period of industrialization as a whole.

The first interpretation might be described as the viewpoint of 'traditional modernism'. Writers like Roger Fry and Clive Bell, whom you encountered in Unit 16, Part 1 *What is Art?,* believed that modern art enshrined the 'classic' (Fry) or 'primitive' (Bell) qualities of the art of previous periods in styles appropriate to the expression of a contemporary sensibility. Modern art was thus defended by drawing attention to the enduring importance of 'form' in art (as opposed, for example, to the 'story-telling' functions exploited by such nineteenth-century artists as the members of the Pre-Raphaelite Brotherhood. See Units 22–23, Section 4.) Though the English art of the nineteenth century was generally condemned as 'illustrative' or 'descriptive' by these traditional modernists, they were concerned to emphasize that there was a larger continuity, a continuity of values, in the history of art, and that modern artists like Cézanne, Picasso and Matisse were the guardians of fundamental qualities of civilization which had been undervalued during the period of industrial expansion.

Fry and Bell objected not so much to the physical effects of industrialization as to the values which they felt were upheld by those with an interest in commerce. Fry contrasted the 'imaginative life' favourably with the 'instinctive life' (in his 'Essay in Aesthetics' published in 1909, the latter part of which is printed in the Supplementary Texts pp. 105–8) and referred to millionaires as 'the Lords of the instinctive life' (in an essay on 'Art and Socialism' first published in 1912). He also criticized Ruskin as a 'moralist' who believed that the 'imaginative life' was subservient to morality. In fastidious reaction against what they saw as the materialism of the nineteenth century, Fry and Bell promoted the value of 'pure disinterested contemplation' such as they associated with experience of art which had what Bell called 'significant form'. Clive Bell's concept of the value of art was strongly influenced by the writings of the philosopher G. E. Moore, who, in his *Principia Ethica* (first published in 1903) expressed the view that '. . . certain states of consciousness, which may be roughly described as the pleasures of human intercourse and the enjoyment of beautiful objects . . . form the rational ultimate end of human action and the sole criterion of social progress.' Bell later wrote of Moore that he had provided deliverance 'from the spell of an ugly doctrine in which we had been reared: he delivered us from Utilitarianism'. (Bell, *Old Friends: Personal Reflections.*)

In opposition to such interpretations were men whose modernism, at its crudest, was expressed in terms of an aggressive enthusiasm for the effects of industrialization, a deliberate exploitation of the imagery of mechanization, and a rejection of the humanistic tradition, characteristically expressed in contempt for 'The Fat Man of the Renaissance' (the phrase comes from a statement written by the painter David Bomberg for the catalogue of a one-man show in 1914).

Though they might have agreed with the traditional modernists that there were 'fundamental qualities' common to the great art of every period, this second group of artists and writers, whom I will characterize as 'radical modernists', celebrated art not so much for its renewal of traditional values as for its capacity to express an essentially modern sensibility. The most extreme and outspoken of the radical modernists were the Italian Futurist writers and artists. The very name they gave themselves suggests an impatience for change. The First Futurist Manifesto was written by the poet F. T. Marinetti and was published in Paris in 1909. Here is a sample of its rhetoric:

> We declare that the splendour of the world has been enriched with a new form of beauty, the beauty of speed. A race-automobile adorned with great pipes like serpents with explosive breath . . . a race-automobile which seems to rush over exploding powder is more beautiful than the *Victory of Samothrace*. . . .
>
> We will glorify war – the only true hygiene of the world – militarism, patriotism, the destructive gesture of the anarchist, the beautiful Ideas which kill, and the scorn of woman.
>
> We will destroy museums, libraries, and fight against moralism, feminism, and all utilitarian cowardice.
>
> We will sing the great masses agitated by work, pleasure or revolt; we will sing the multicoloured and polyphonic surf of revolutions in modern capitals; the nocturnal vibration of arsenals and docks beneath their glaring electric moons; greedy stations devouring smoking serpents; factories hanging from clouds by the threads of their smoke; bridges like giant gymnasts stepping over sunny rivers sparkling like diabolical cutlery; adventurous steamers scenting the horizon; large-breasted locomotives bridled with long tubes; and the slippery flight of airplanes whose propellers have flaglike flutterings and applauses of enthusiastic crowds. (Translation made under Marinetti's direction, published in the catalogue of an exhibition of Futurist painting in London, 1912.)

The imagery of the Manifesto is determinedly 'modern', but you might try re-reading the passage above in the light of the encyclopedia entry for Romanticism quoted in Unit 21. It seems to me that the passage I've quoted exhibits many characteristics identifiable as romantic: an emphasis on 'imagination and emotion over reason and intellect', a bizarre form of idealism, 'revolt against political authority and social convention', the 'cultivation of emotion and sensation for their own sakes', and an attraction to the cruel. There is also, I would say, an equivalent for the romantic's 'nature worship' in the fevered enthusiasm for racing-cars, steamers, locomotives and planes, described as if they were living creatures. For all the Futurists' propagandizing of a break with the past, there is surely a continuity of ideas and of means of expressing them. Perhaps what I've called radical modernism is really the terminal expression of a sensibility which has its origins in the eighteenth century.

Whether that's so or not, it is surely clear that the Futurists were concerned to glorify the 'power of willing' and that they associated wilful action in the modern world with concepts like speed and energy. The element of abstraction in the works of the radical modernist painters was characteristically designed to embody some form of energy – to convey a quality rather than to represent certain forms. You might like to look back at the illustration of the Futurist Boccioni's *States of Mind; the Farewells,* printed in Unit 18, *Art and Visual Perception. Form and Meaning,* and the painting by Balla which is reproduced here as Figure 6.

The typical radical modernist saw an interest in Nature, in the sense celebrated by the nineteenth-century landscape painter, as inconsistent with an acceptance of the 'realities' of modern life. 'Nature is a blessed retreat, in art, for those

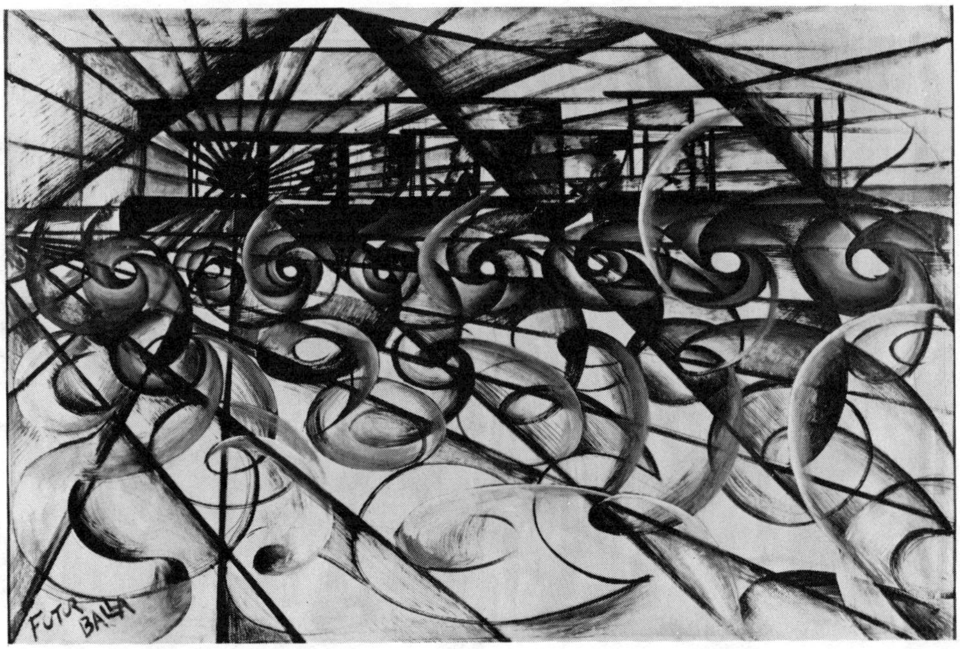

Figure 6 Giacomo Balla Abstract Speed: Wake of Speeding Automobile, *oil, $20\frac{1}{8} \times 25\frac{1}{2}$", 1913 (Private Collection).*

artists whose imagination is mean and feeble, whose Vocation and instinct are unrobust.' That was written by Percy Wyndham Lewis, the most energetic and articulate of the radical modernist painters in England, the leader of a group known as the Vorticists, and the driving force behind the publication of a magazine called *Blast*.

There were two issues of *Blast*, in 1914 and 1915 respectively. I reproduce a page from the first issue (Figure 7) together with two woodcuts by the Vorticist painter Edward Wadsworth (Figures 8 and 9).

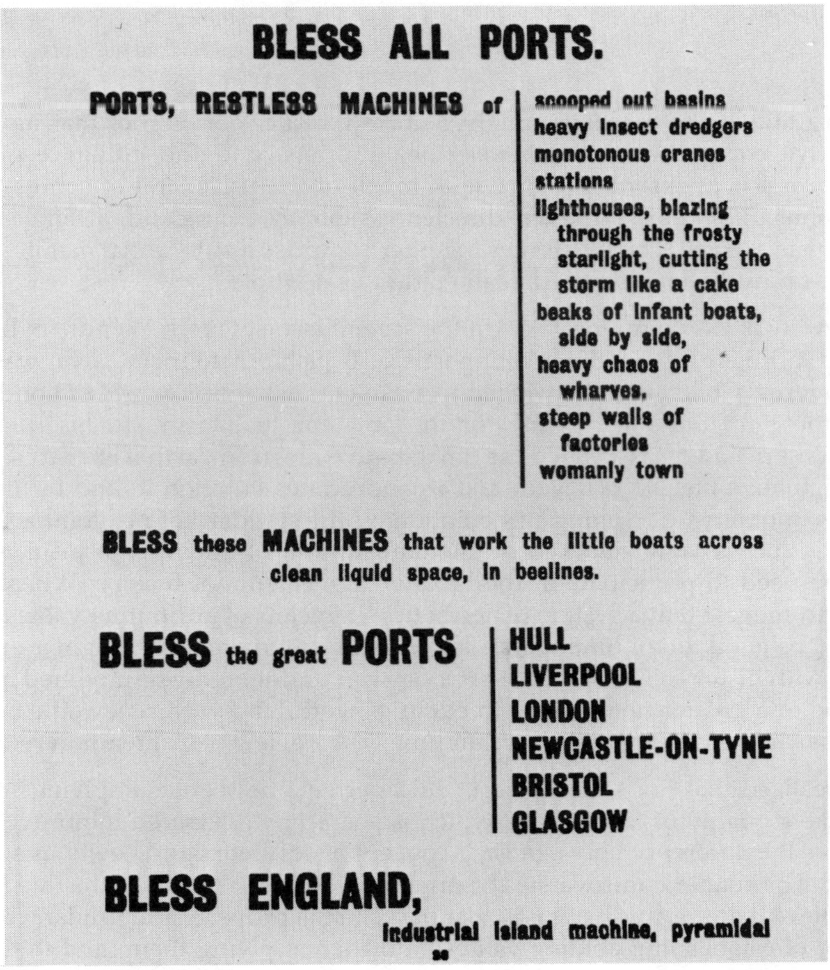

BLESS ALL PORTS.

PORTS, RESTLESS MACHINES of

scooped out basins
heavy insect dredgers
monotonous cranes
stations
lighthouses, blazing through the frosty starlight, cutting the storm like a cake
beaks of infant boats, side by side,
heavy chaos of wharves,
steep walls of factories
womanly town

BLESS these **MACHINES** that work the little boats across clean liquid space, in beelines.

BLESS the great **PORTS**

HULL
LIVERPOOL
LONDON
NEWCASTLE-ON-TYNE
BRISTOL
GLASGOW

BLESS ENGLAND,

industrial island machine, pyramidal

Figure 7 Page 23 of Blast, *No. 1, 20 June 1914.*

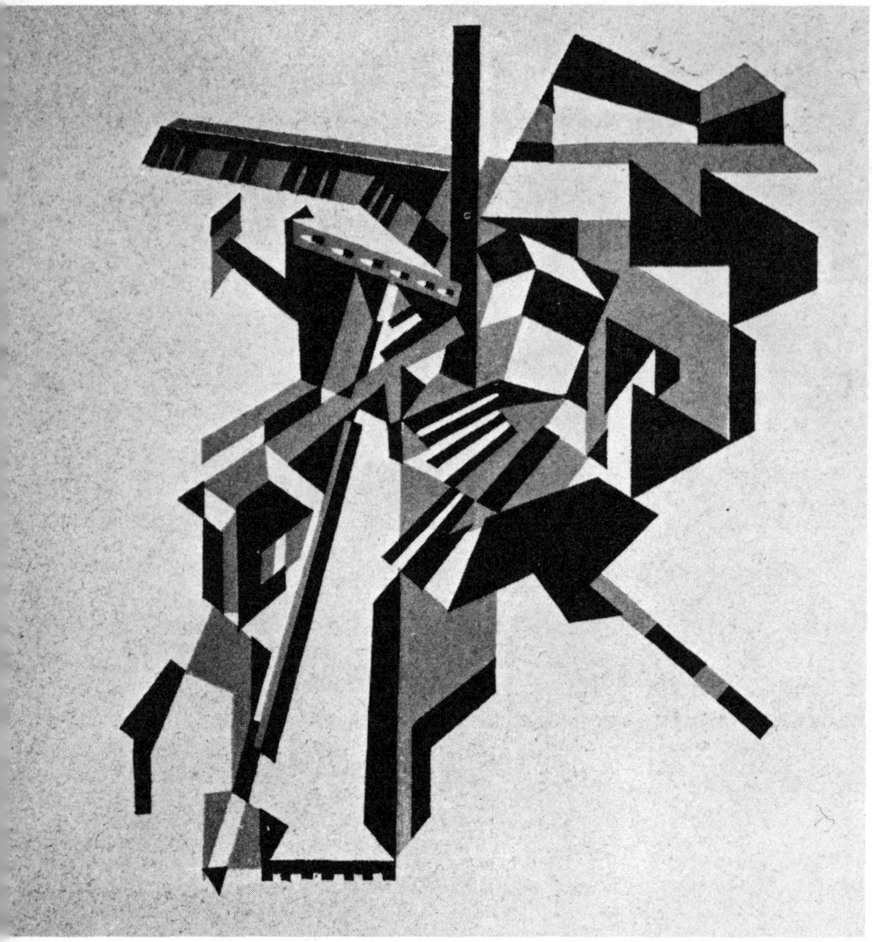

Figure 8 Edward Wadsworth, Mytholmroyd, *woodcut, 8½ × 7", c. 1914 (Whitworth Art Gallery, University of Manchester).*

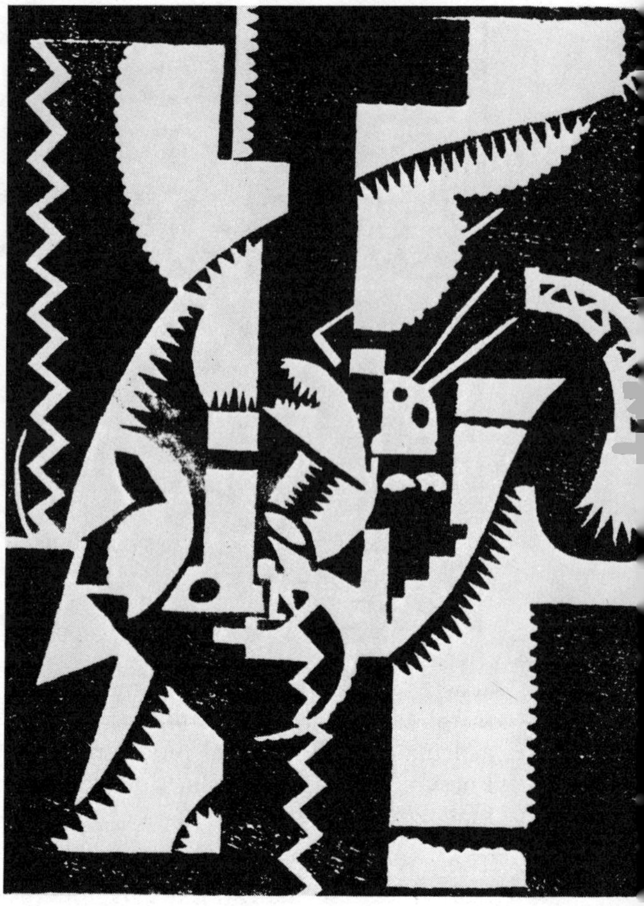

Figure 9 Edward Wadsworth Newcastle, *woodcut, 5½ × 4", 1913 (Photo from* Blast, *No. 1, 20 June 1914, page 29).*

The very title of the magazine might be taken as a celebration of that modern destructive energy which fascinated the Futurists, and the influence of the Italian group is apparent in the style of much of the prose and of some of the illustrations. *Blast* was, however, directed essentially at England, at English art and English society. The two issues together comprise a substantial manifesto of modernism in the context of English culture as a whole.

In a 'Review of Contemporary Art' in the second issue of *Blast*, Wyndham Lewis referred to Roger Fry as 'the great apostle of British amateurism', who was 'all for the eternal Child and who wished to make of the painting-world of London a tight little right little world safe for the amateur to live in'. In his *Essay in Aesthetics,* Fry had disassociated the 'imaginative life' from 'actual life'; art serves the imaginative life, he believed, and it 'appreciates emotion in and for itself', whereas 'morality . . . appreciates emotion by the standard of resultant action'. To Lewis such a view smacked of dilettantism and of attempts to insulate art from the need to participate in the broader movements of history. Where Fry tended to suggest that a system of aesthetics – a means of attributing value to art – should be good for all time, Lewis felt that the criteria for criticism in art must change with history: 'The whole of art today can undoubtedly be modified in the direction of a greater imaginative freedom of work, and with renewed conception of aesthetics in sympathy with our time.' ('A Review of Contemporary Art'.)

Lewis realized that Fry's view of art could perhaps be seen as implying something like a quality of 'good taste' which is shared by a leisured minority. One might see the difference between Fry's concept of aesthetics and Lewis' as symptomatic of a broader controversy: the argument between those on the one hand who believe that the study of history or of culture is properly and fundamentally a matter of establishing abiding values, and then applying them, and those on the other who believe that one's terms of reference must inevitably change, not only in relation to different subjects of study but also in response to (or as part of) the inexorable historical and cultural changes which are taking place while such studies progress.

I'd like to look briefly at a drawing by Wyndham Lewis (Figure 10) and in more detail at a sculpture by Jacob Epstein (Figures 11 and 12 and cover), who was an associate of Lewis and whose work was illustrated in *Blast*. Each of these artists was concerned to provide an image of man which would embody a distinctively 'modern' quality, and each interpreted this quality (i.e. provided an image of man's nature) in terms of imagery drawn from the appearance of machines.

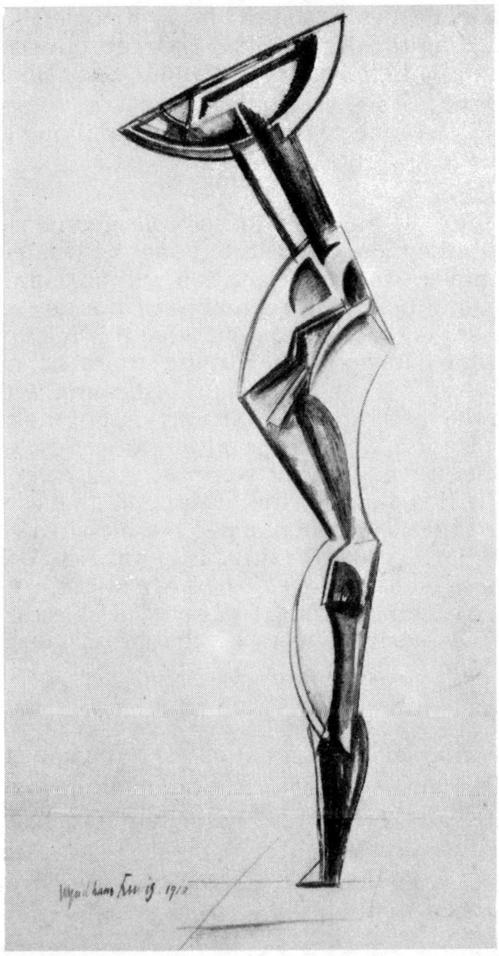

Figure 10 Wyndham Lewis The Enemy of the Stars, *pen and ink, 17¼ ×7⅞", 1913 (Anthony d'Offay Gallery).*

EXERCISE

Could you find grounds to compare or contrast this strange image with any of the illustrations in Units 22–23, *Nature, Work and Art,* for example Millet's *Man with a Hoe* (Figure 59) or Van Gogh's *Miner with a Shovel* (Figure 74)? I should perhaps say that I don't think there'd be much point in comparing or contrasting them in terms of their formal appearance.

DISCUSSION

What is perhaps significant is that Lewis' drawing looks only as human as it has to in order that we shall see it as a figure of some sort. Where Millet and Van Gogh were picturing individuals in such a way that we can see them as representatives of types (the agricultural or the industrial labourer), Lewis seems to be attempting to create something quite different: an image embodying certain qualities of a very general sort, such as tension, dynamic balance, hardness etc., which are also found as characteristics of machinery. Where Millet and Van Gogh might be said to be drawing attention to certain aspects of the lives of individual people, Lewis appears to be seeking an image which will stand for the kind of 'modern energy' which he admires. It is significant that this image is one which could surely not be classified as 'humanistic'.

The most articulate and sympathetic of radical modernist writers in England was the philosopher T. E. Hulme. Here is what he wrote, in 1914, about Lewis' drawings:

> It is obvious that the artist's only interest in the human body was in a few abstract mechanical relations perceived in it, the arm as lever and so on. The interest in living flesh as such, in all that detail that makes it vital, which is pleasing, and which we like to see reproduced, is entirely absent. ('Modern Art and its Philosophy' in Hulme, *Speculations*.)

Hulme saw the art of Lewis and of Epstein as exemplifying a 'tendency towards abstraction' which, he believed, would

> . . . culminate, not so much in the simple geometrical forms found in archaic art, but in the more complicated ones associated in our minds with the idea of machinery. In this association with machinery will probably be found the specific differentiating quality of the new art. It is difficult to define properly at the present moment what this relation to machinery will be. It has nothing whatever to do with the superficial notion that one must beautify machinery. It is not a question of dealing with machinery in the spirit, and with the methods of existing art, but of the creation of a new art having an organization, and governed by principles, which are at present exemplified unintentionally, as it were, in machinery. It is hardly necessary to repeat at this stage of the argument, that it will not aim at the satisfaction of that particular mental need, which in a vital art results in the production of what is called beauty. It is aiming at the satisfaction of a different mental need altogether. When Mr Roger Fry, therefore, talks as he did lately of 'machinery being as beautiful as a rose' he demonstrates what is already obvious from his work, that he has no conception whatever of this new art, and is in fact a mere verbose sentimentalist. ('Modern Art and its Philosophy.')

This may seem like a rational explanation of the appearance of modern art, but the published form of Hulme's 'Modern Art and its Philosophy', from which the quotation is drawn, is prefaced by the following sentence: 'The fright of the mind before the unknown created not only the first gods, but also the first art.' This seems to suggest a view that the motivation for art is irrational. We catch here another echo of that modernist romanticism which was so strong in the Futurists and Vorticists and which is, I believe, a consistent feature of all radical modernism.

'Philosophy', Hulme once wrote, as if to explain his own inability to contribute much to the subject, 'is about people in clothes and not about the soul of man'. (From 'Cinders; a sketch of a new Weltanschauung' in *Speculations*.)

Along with their interest in the imagery of an industrialized world many artists and critics in the early years of the century showed a strong fascination with the concept of the primitive and with the art of 'primitive' peoples. (Aaron Scharf quoted Fry's essay on 'Negro Sculpture' in Unit 16.) The two interests came together in the art and writing of the radical modernists. Wyndham Lewis wrote of men as primitives in the 'iron jungle' of the modern metropolis (in *Blast* 2), and of machines as reflecting man's basic violent nature. Following Wilhelm Worringer, a German writer on aesthetics, Hulme believed that all art could be characterized either as 'geometric' or as 'vital'. (This latter term might be taken to mean roughly the same as 'organic'; i.e. having some of the formal characteristics of living things.) He saw primitive art as crudely geometric, while the humanistic styles which characterized Greek, Renaissance and post-Renaissance art were labelled as 'vital'. He believed that 'the re-emergence of geometrical art may be the precursor of the re-emergence of the corresponding attitude towards the world, and so of the break up of the Renaissance humanistic attitude'. Again following Worringer, Hulme interpreted the modern tendency to abstraction as a symptom of unease in man's relation to the natural world. The 'different mental need' which he referred to in the longer passage quoted above was for intense and intuitive self-assertion in a world experienced as chaotic.

Hulme had associated primitivism, anti-humanism and 'the idea of machinery' in an attempt both to characterize the prevailing sensibility of modern culture and to suggest that this sensibility was different in kind rather than in quality from that of the centuries since the Renaissance. One of the most forceful expressions of this sensibility was provided by Hulme's close friend Jacob Epstein in his sculpture known as the *Rock Drill*. I illustrate a preparatory drawing of 1913 and a recent reconstruction of the completed sculpture as it was when exhibited in March 1915 (Figures 11 and 12).

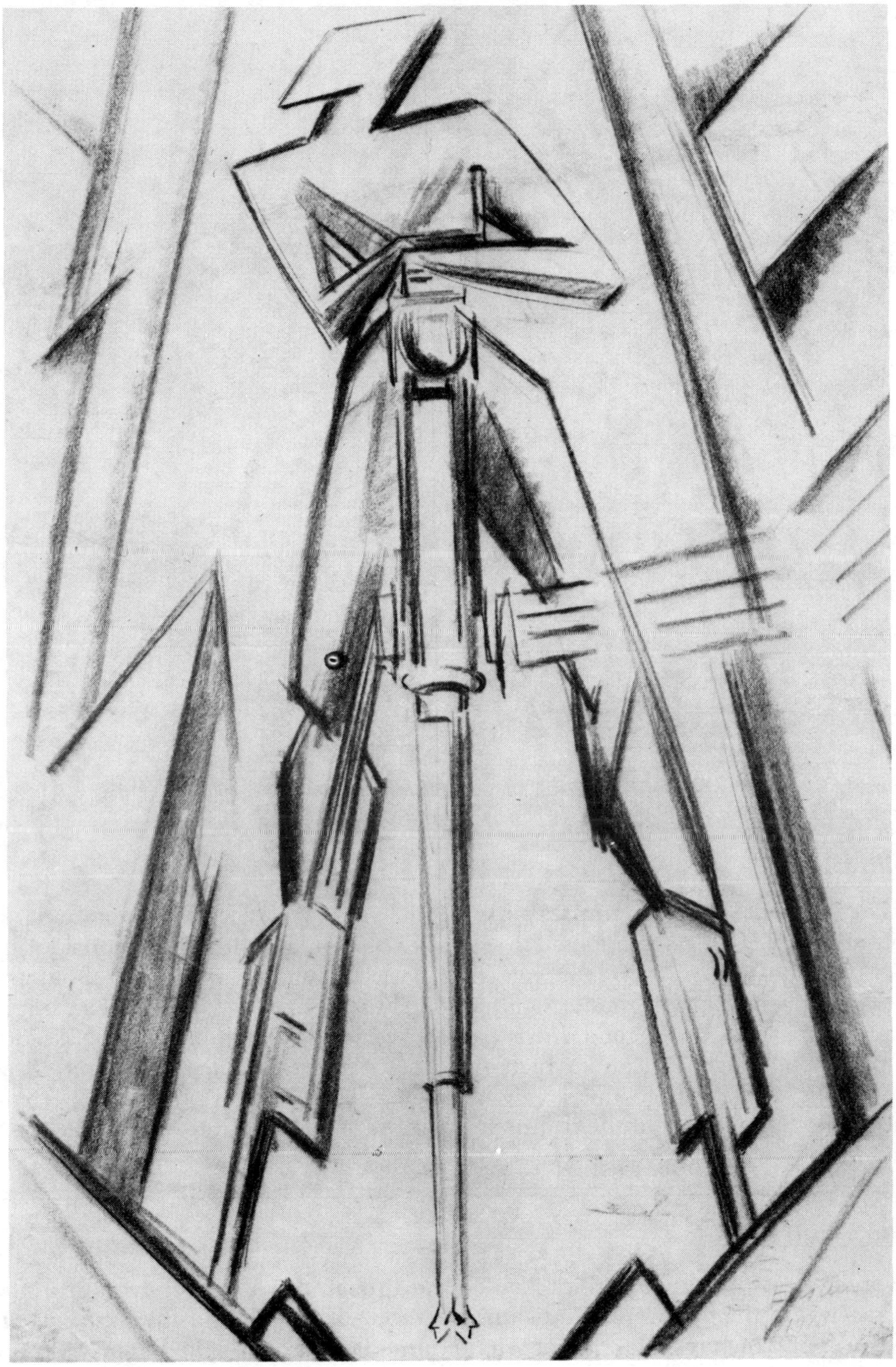

Figure 11 Jacob Epstein Study for 'Rock Drill' *(front), crayon, 27⅙ × 16⅔", 1913 (Anthony d'Offay Gallery).*

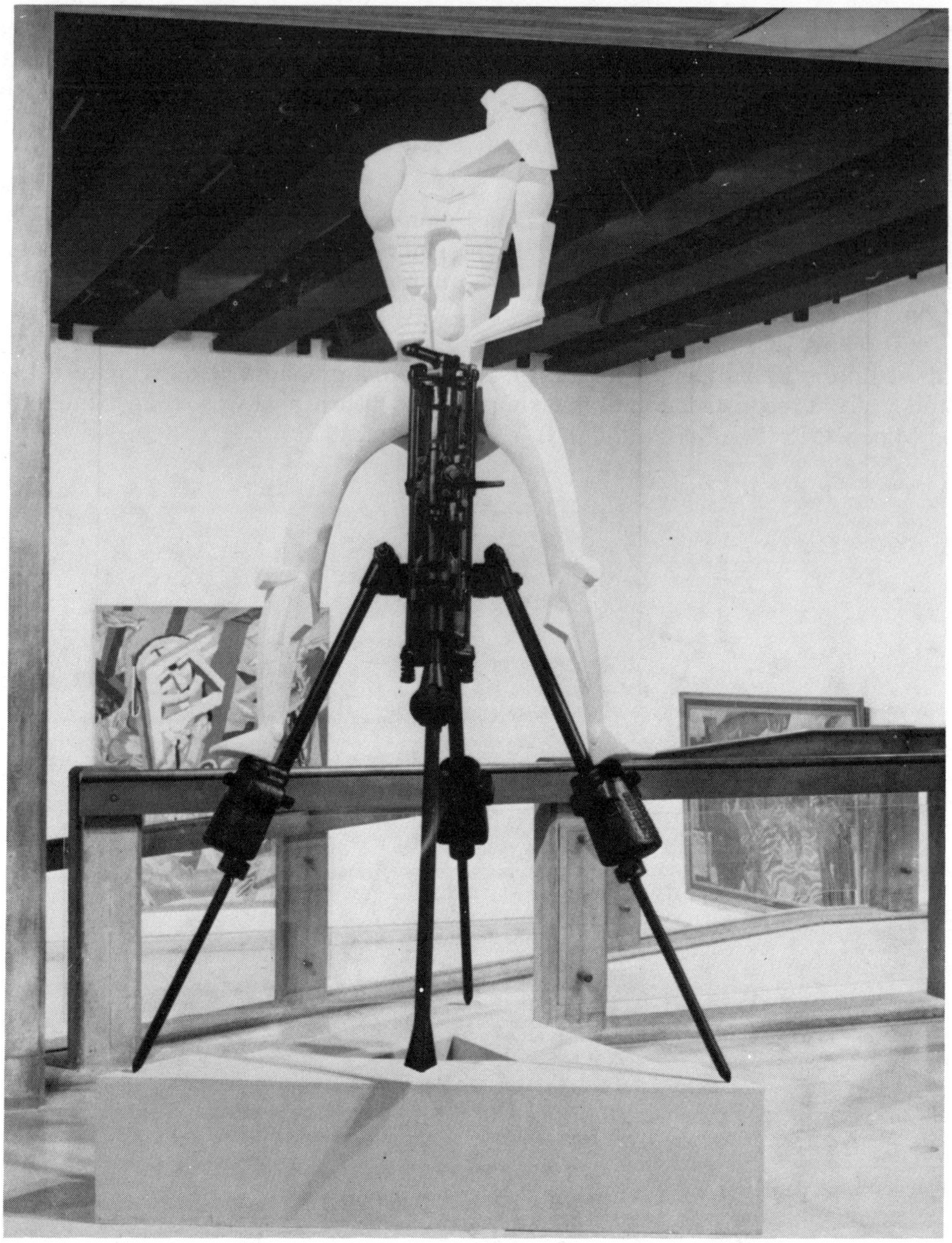

Figure 12 Reconstruction of 'Rock Drill', 1974. *(Photo from negative supplied by Anthony Dawson. Reproduced by courtesy of the Arts Council of Great Britain.)*

EXERCISE

Make a note of your own impressions of this work. What seems to you remarkable about it? Does it seem to you to express a particular attitude? (In considering this last question, rather than referring back to what I have said about the prevailing sensibility of modern culture as characterized by Hulme, you might like to look back to Léger's *Three Women*, which is illustrated in the Colour Supplement (page 13), and which Aaron Scharf characterized in Unit 18 as 'optimistic' and as suggesting a view of the machine as 'man's benefactor'.) You should bear in mind that the completed sculpture was about ten feet high overall.

DISCUSSION

I would expect you to have remarked on the appearance of aggressiveness in the work and on the apparently anti-human, robot-like quality of the figure itself, the form of which is certainly not what Hulme would have called 'vital'. On the other hand there is an awkwardness about the combination of sculptured figure (made out of plaster) and real metal drill, though this is perhaps not as apparent from the photo as it must have been in front of the work itself. You might have guessed that the size of the work would have increased its overpowering effect on the spectator. (The contemporary critic of the *Evening News* described it as 'a nightmare in plaster, a kind of gigantic human locust, all angles and curves and flat surfaces, a cubist-futurist abortion of indescribably revolting aspect'. You may well agree with him.) In relation to Léger's picture of human figures apparently at one with a modern post-industrial environment, Epstein's view appears surely more alarming. The machine has become an analogy for man, and the machine's functions a grim metaphor for his own. Wyndham Lewis described the sculpture as 'a vivid illustration of the greatest function of life' (in a review of the London Group exhibition published in *Blast* 2). As the drawing makes clear, the *Rock Drill* is a symbol of potency, a parthenogenetic sexual potency which is far from tender. The sculpture might be described as a fetish of energy, seen as both a modern mechanical and a primitive human quality.

The First World War was in progress when the *Rock Drill* was first exhibited, and it was perhaps inevitable that the sculpture should have been interpreted in the light of current events. A photo of the sculpture was published by the *Daily Graphic* in May 1915 under the headline 'War as the Futurist sees it'. In fact Epstein would not have called himself a Futurist, and the date of the drawing makes clear that the idea for the sculpture was formulated well before the outbreak of war, while the entire work was probably complete by the end of 1913. In 1913–14 revolution was contemplated more often and more readily than war by some people in England.

Epstein himself seems to have come to see the *Rock Drill* as a sinister and pessimistic figure, but I'm not sure that he originally considered the work in such terms. The following is a passage from his autobiography, *Let there be Sculpture*, published years later in 1940.

> It was in the experimental pre-war days of 1913 that I was fired to do the rock drill, and my ardour for machinery (short-lived) expended itself upon the purchase of an actual drill, second-hand, and upon this I made and mounted a machine-like robot, visored, menacing, and carrying within itself its progeny, protectively ensconced. Here is the armed, sinister figure of to-day and to-morrow. No humanity, only the terrible Frankenstein's monster we have made ourselves into.

The Great War blighted many hopes and destroyed many ideals, and I think it is likely that the realization that this most unartistic outburst of 'modern destructive energy' was the real outcome of recent history was influential in causing Epstein, like many other of the pre-war radical modernists, to change his views on the modern world, and thus to modify the style of his work. In 1916 he truncated his remarkable sculpture, discarding the drill and cutting the figure down to size as it were, thus reducing it to something that could be accommodated on a conventional plinth. The torso was then cast in bronze (see cover illustration). 'Murder and destruction is man's fundamental occupation', wrote Wyndham Lewis (in *Blast* 2) before departing for the war.

Perhaps in response to the disappointment of their hopes of the modern world, the pre-war radical modernists became comparatively conservative figures in the post-war years. As Lewis wrote in 1939, 'The brave new world was a mirage – a snare and a delusion' ('The Skeleton in the Cupboard speaks', in *Wyndham Lewis the Artist from Blast to Burlington House*). There was little taste for experiment in the art of the early 1920s; the representative English artist turned away from the characteristic features of modern technology towards still-life and landscape themes. The industrial world appeared, for the time being, to have lost its fascination.

Certain questions have dogged the history of modern art since the end of the Great War. How does the artist engage with the modern world? Is it a matter of selecting his subject matter from among the products of industrial development?

Or is it a matter rather of transmitting a distinctively 'modern sensibility' through his work? If the latter, how is this sensibility to be identified and distinguished as modern? For many people – perhaps a majority – 'modern art' means things that look odd and incomprehensible. Does this oddness, this incomprehensibility, signify an inability or unwillingness on the modern artist's part to be realistic, to engage the world in some definite way? Or is the very strangeness of the work a measure of his intuition of reality? Is the individuality of his vision the measure of its value? Or is it merely a symptom of the artist's isolation in a world where the nature of his relations with those around him has been transformed by the consequences of industrialization?

As a conclusion to this section, I reproduce a work by an artist whose paintings, perhaps more than any other's, have come to be taken as representative of the consequences of industrialization as they are experienced in this country in the twentieth century (Figure 13).

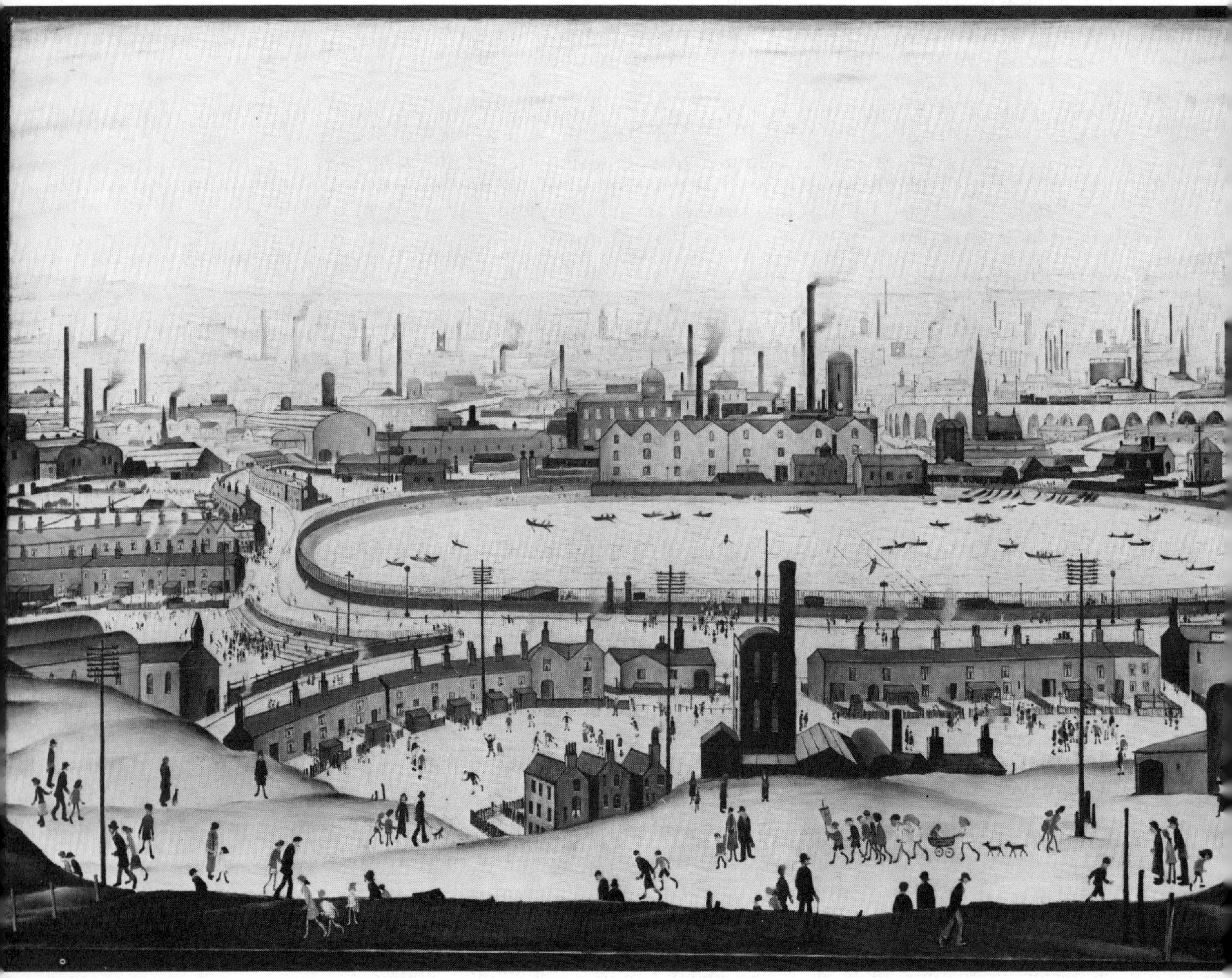

Figure 13 L. S. Lowry The Pond, *oil, 45 × 60", 1950 (Tate Gallery, London).*

EXERCISE

What view of industrialization and its effects do you think is expressed in this painting?

DISCUSSION

L. S. Lowry reflects none of the enthusiasm, the idealism of the early modernists; indeed his work exhibits few of the characteristics normally associated with modernism. But when an artist's work achieves wide acceptance, as Lowry's has, it is usually because a great many people believe that the pictures he paints are 'realistic' in some sense. The questions we should ask, I think, are these. Is Lowry's picture of life in a typical industrial town a *true* picture? How do we decide upon its truth or falsity? Can we be sure that we are not merely seeking confirmation of our own opinions as to the 'quality of life' in industrial Lancashire or wherever?

My own view, for what it's worth, is that Lowry offers a 'negative idealization', a picture which pleases by confirming certain pessimistic assumptions while at the same time reflecting a picturesque world, where unreal antlike figures stand in for the actual occupants of the industrial landscape. The 'quality of life' evoked is surely a fantasy. The picture over-simplifies, to the point of falsehood, those aspects of life in an industrialized society which testify to real alienation or real community.

PART 3 D. H. LAWRENCE

What does the name 'D. H. Lawrence' suggest to you? His famous, at one time notorious, novel *Lady Chatterley's Lover*? Or more vaguely, the man who wrote novels making 'a religion of sex'? Or less vaguely, the equally famous novel, *Sons and Lovers*, about life in a Nottinghamshire colliery village? Or perhaps only the author of 'the book of the film' of a few years ago, *Women in Love,* starring Alan Bates and Glenda Jackson? But however much or little you know about Lawrence, it's likely to centre on the fact that he *was* a novelist, which raises, or should raise, the question for you – why introduce him at this late stage of the course? What has a twentieth-century novelist to say about the theme of the last twelve units, 'Arts and Society in an Age of Industrialization'? As it turns out, a great deal and that is one good reason for a brief discussion of his thought. Another is, precisely, that he belongs to the twentieth century,

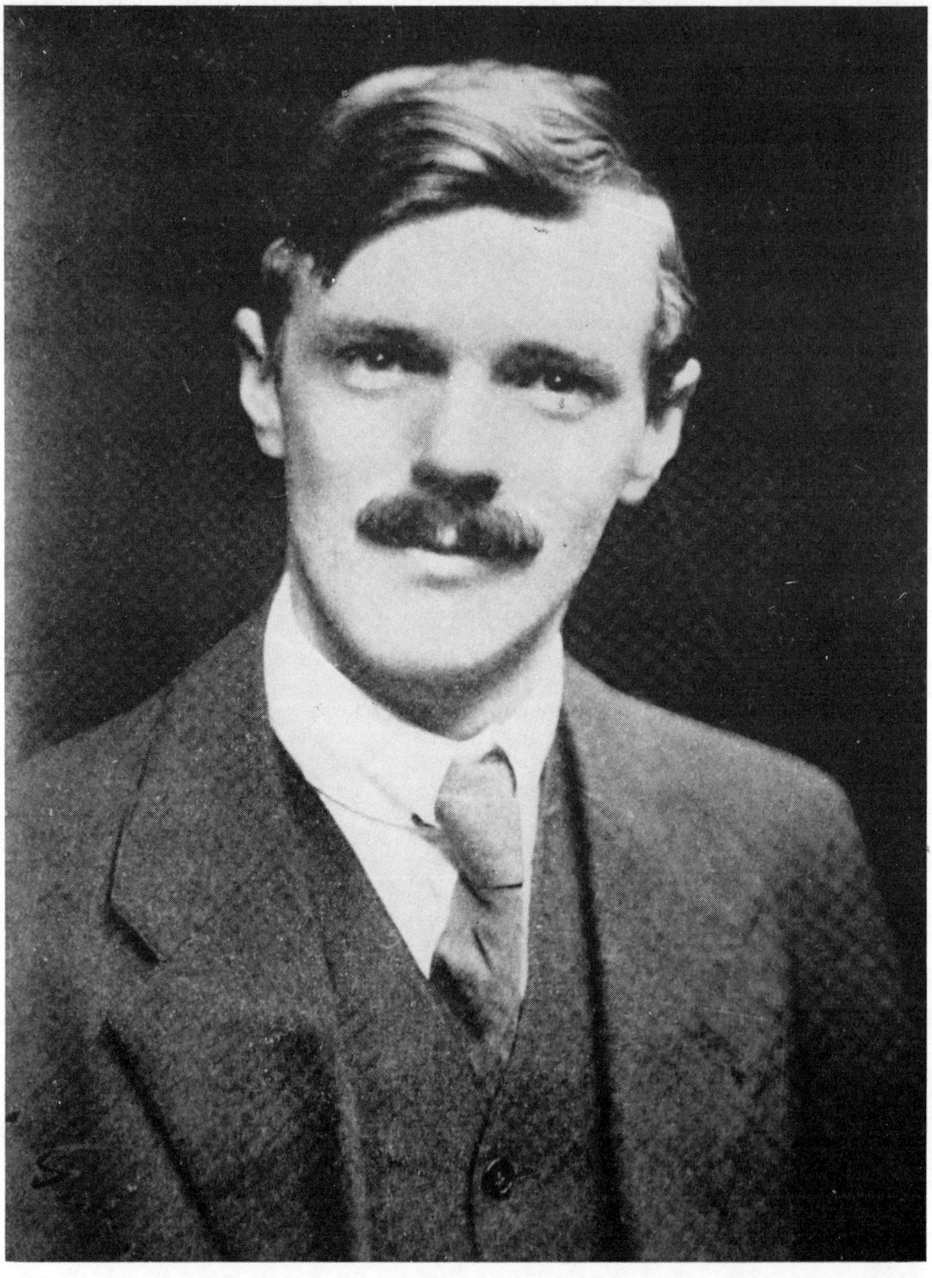

Figure 14 D. H. Lawrence in 1913. (Photo supplied by Local Studies Library, Nottinghamshire County Library. Reproduced by courtesy of David Garnett.)

which underlines the relevance of the theme of these units to our own time. Of course, today's problems are not those of the nineteenth century, if only because we're not experiencing for the first time that astounding transformation of the world that we call 'industrialization'. But our way of seeing these problems, our intellectual concepts for grappling them, the cultural reverberations which reflect our attempts to define their human meaning, all these owe much to the nineteenth-century debate. Lawrence's restatement of the problems, as he felt them, has its twentieth-century aspect, but it also draws on some of the ideas you've already met in previous units.

There's a third reason for introducing Lawrence. Much of what he wrote in the first decades of this century (he died in 1930) seems today to have a prophetic ring. Lawrence exemplifies a strange general characteristic of the arts, that they sometimes find a way of talking about hidden forces at work in a society, creating a new language for truths not yet generally apparent. Lawrence sensed tendencies within English, and indeed within European and American, society of the years 1910–30, that we are only today beginning fully to understand. We now realize that we have the scientific knowledge and technological power to destroy, not just human societies, but the world of nature itself. Since Hiroshima 1945, we have had to live with that nightmarish possibility. It's not too much to say of Lawrence that he prophesied it.

Prophets usually sound eccentric in their own time. They exaggerate. They get over-excited. They have no sense of proportion, no patience with our usual cautious routines for deciding the truth or untruth of an assertion. They're awkward customers all round. And Lawrence was no exception. Aldous Huxley tells the following story about Lawrence, whom he knew well in the 1920s, and greatly admired:

> Lawrence disapproved of too much knowledge, on the score that it diminished men's sense of wonder and blunted their sensitiveness to the great mystery. His dislike of science was passionate and expressed itself in the most fantastically unreasonable terms. 'All scientists are liars', he would say, when I brought up some experimentally established fact, which he happened to dislike. 'Liars, liars!' It was a most convenient theory. I remember in particular one long and violent argument on evolution, in the reality of which Lawrence always passionately disbelieved. 'But look at the evidence, Lawrence', I insisted, 'look at all the evidence.' His answer was characteristic. 'But I don't care about evidence. Evidence doesn't mean anything to me. I don't feel it *here*.' And he pressed his two hands on his solar plexus. (*Letters*, pp. xiv–xv.)

Not, of course, an impressive argument, and it certainly didn't impress Huxley. In his talks with Lawrence he learned to avoid the whole question of scientific truth, deciding that it was pointless to expend energy battling with obdurate prejudices when Lawrence had so much else to give. Lawrence believed that knowledge of the world had to be 'living' if it was to be valuable. He hated what he called 'mental knowledge', a merely knowing-about things, as distinct from immediately sensing their concrete existence, their 'otherness'. His passionate dismissal of scientific evidence stemmed from a conviction that it wasn't a knowledge of living systems known by living men, but of abstractions, a shadow-world known merely 'in the head', which then came between living men and their potential for direct experience.

Huxley goes on:

> To be with Lawrence was a kind of adventure, a voyage of discovery into newness and otherness . . . A walk with him in the country was a walk through that marvellously rich and significant landscape which is at once the background and the principal personage of all his novels. He seemed to know, by personal experience, what it was like to be a tree or a daisy or a breaking wave or even the mysterious moon itself. He could get inside the skin of an animal and tell you in the most convincing detail how it felt and how, dimly, inhumanly it thought . . . To be with him was to find oneself transported to one of the frontiers of human consciousness. For an inhabitant of the safe metropolis of thought and feeling it was a most exciting experience. (*Letters*, pp. xxx–xxxi.)

Huxley felt that Lawrence was an explorer *beyond* what was already known about the world. So perhaps we shouldn't be too surprised at Lawrence's hostility towards science which, at any one point in time, is always concerned to organize *what is already known* into a coherent logically-linked system. Genuinely new knowledge, as distinct from some extension of the logical implications of present knowledge, always has to fight its way. In the middle of the nineteenth century, everybody envisaged atoms, the ultimate units of matter, as tiny billiard balls, impenetrably hard. A scientist who had said 'Rubbish! Atoms aren't solid at all. They're mainly empty space, concentrations of electrical energy into a sort of nucleus surrounded by whirling electrons' wouldn't have got much of a hearing. Of course, that is not to compare Lawrence's rejection of science with the discoveries of twentieth-century physics, but simply to remind you that knowledge advances by processes of challenge and contradiction, and that sometimes the discontinuities are abrupt. What was this new knowledge of the world that Lawrence preferred to scientific truth?

Here is an extract from a letter he wrote in 1919 when he was staying in a cottage in Derbyshire.

> Yesterday I went out for a real walk – I've had a cold and been in bed. I climbed with my niece to the bare top of the hills. Wonderful it is to see the footmarks on the snow – beautiful ropes of rabbit prints, trailing away over the brows; heavy hare marks; a fox, so sharp and dainty, going over the wall: birds with two feet that hop; very splendid straight advance of a pheasant; wood-pigeons that are clumsy and move in flocks; splendid little leaping marks of weasels, coming along like a necklace chain of berries; odd little filigree of the field-mice; the trail of a mole – it is astonishing what a world of wild creatures one feels around one, on the hills in the snow. From the height it is very beautiful. The upland is naked, white like silver, and moving far into the distance, strange and muscular, with gleams like skin. Only the wind surprises one, invisibly cold; the sun lies bright on a field, like the movement of a sleeper. It is strange how insignificant in all this life seems. Two men, tiny as dots, move from a farm on a snow slope, carrying hay to the beasts. Every moment they seem to melt like insignificant spots of dust; the sheer, living, muscular white of the uplands absorbs everything. Only there is a tiny clump of trees bare on the hill-top – small beeches – writhing like iron in the blue sky. – I wish one could cease to be a human being, and be a demon. (*Letters*, 468–9.)

What do you think of that? Read it through again. Then write down two points about it, one connecting it with what Huxley said about Lawrence in the second quotation, the other noting the main surprise in the passage.

DISCUSSION

The description of the scene illustrates very directly Huxley's experience of a walk in the country with Lawrence. The details speak for themselves. The scene comes to life in a marvellously vivid way. We don't simply *see* the bird and animal tracks. We sense the different kinds of movement that caused them. We feel the cold air, the shape and movement of the snow-covered land. What I meant by a 'surprise' is surely in the conclusion, Lawrence's wish to lose his human identity. The human beings in the landscape are the least significant things in it. Even his own presence as an observer offends him.

Now read this poem, considering it again in relation to the second Huxley quotation. Does it surprise you in any way?

Snake
A snake came to my water-trough
On a hot, hot day, and I in pyjamas for the heat,
To drink there.

In the deep, strange-scented shade of the great dark carob-tree
I came down the steps with my pitcher
And must wait, must stand and wait, for there he was at the trough before me.

He reached down from a fissure in the earth-wall in the gloom
And trailed his yellow-brown slackness soft-bellied down, over the edge of the stone trough
And rested his throat upon the stone bottom,
And where the water had dripped from the tap, in a small clearness,
He sipped with his straight mouth,
Softly drank through his straight gums, into his slack long body,
Silently.

Someone was before me at my water-trough,
And I, like a second comer, waiting.

He lifted his head from his drinking, as cattle do,
And looked at me vaguely, as drinking cattle do,
And flickered his two-forked tongue from his lips, and mused a moment,
And stooped and drank a little more,
Being earth-brown, earth-golden from the burning bowels of the earth
On the day of Sicilian July, with Etna smoking.

The voice of my education said to me
He must be killed,
For in Sicily the black, black snakes are innocent, the gold are venomous.

And voices in me said, If you were a man
You would take a stick and break him now, and finish him off.

But must I confess how I liked him,
How glad I was he had come like a guest in quiet, to drink at my water-trough
And depart peaceful, pacified, and thankless,
Into the burning bowels of this earth?

Was it cowardice, that I dared not kill him?
Was it perversity, that I longed to talk to him?
Was it humility, to feel so honoured?
I felt so honoured.

And yet those voices:
If you were not afraid, you would kill him!

And truly I was afraid, I was most afraid,
But even so, honoured still more
That he should seek my hospitality
From out the dark door of the secret earth.

He drank enough
And lifted his head, dreamily, as one who has drunken,
And flickered his tongue like a forked night on the air, so black,
Seeming to lick his lips,
And looked around like a god, unseeing, into the air,
And slowly turned his head,
And slowly, very slowly, as if thrice adream,
Proceeded to draw his slow length curving round
And climb again the broken bank of my wall-face.

And as he put his head into that dreadfule hole,
And as he slowly drew up, snake-easing his shoulders, and entered farther,
A sort of horror, a sort of protest against his withdrawing into that horrid black hole,
Deliberately going into the blackness, and slowly drawing himself after,
Overcame me now his back was turned.

I looked round, I put down my pitcher,
I picked up a clumsy log
And threw it at the water-trough with a clatter.

I think it did not hit him,
But suddenly that part of him that was left behind convulsed in undignified haste,
Writhed like lightning, and was gone
Into the black hole, the earth-lipped fissure in the wall-front,
At which, in the intense still noon, I stared with fascination.

And immediately I regretted it.
I thought how paltry, how vulgar, what a mean act!
I despised myself and the voices of my accursed human education.

And I thought of the albatross,
And I wished he would come back, my snake.

For he seemed to me again like a king,
Like a king in exile, uncrowned in the underworld,
Now due to be crowned again.

And so, I missed my chance with one of the lords
Of life.
And I have something to expiate;
A pettiness.

DISCUSSION

There's the evocation of the creature itself. It is more than a description. Lawrence makes us feel the sinuous muscular movements of the snake as it reaches into the stone trough, sips the water, then turns its head to and fro before withdrawing into the wall. He succeeds in making the creature's actions dignified, mysterious.

He drank enough
And lifted his head, dreamily, as one who has drunken,
And flickered his tongue like a forked night on the air, so black,

Seeming to lick his lips,
And looking around like a god, unseeing, into the air,
And slowly turned his head,
And slowly, very slowly, as if thrice adream,
Proceeded to draw his slow length curving around
And climb again the broken bank of my wall-face.

This inner identification with the snake is an example of what Huxley claimed for Lawrence's knowledge of plants and animals. What is surprising about it? Perhaps there are really two things. Once we've responded to Lawrence's poem we probably forget how remarkably successful he is in setting aside our usual human attitude towards snakes, deriving no doubt from the fact that they're not mammals. With snakes we don't have that obscure sense of a shared world that makes it easy to feel a sort of sympathy for mammals of all kinds, even savage predators. Then, our cultural training, by way of the Garden of Eden story, encourages us to think poorly of snakes. And, perhaps, as a Freudian would say, it is that snakes can symbolize for us the frightening power of sexuality.

Lawrence's poem ignores, or overcomes, all these half-conscious feelings, with the surprisingness of successful art – which seems quite inevitable once it's happened. So it is really a more explicit surprise that I hope you noticed: the end of the poem. Read it again, if you still don't see what I'm after.

DISCUSSION

Lawrence ends by hailing the snake as *'one of the lords of life'*. He despises himself for having given way to 'the voices of my accursed human education' saying snakes should be killed. His poem is more than a description. It is a moral tale. It shows how Lawrence learned something from his encounter with the snake, his own human pettiness and the snake's mysterious dignity even in this simplest of acts, drinking water from a trough. It is, surely, an unexpected lesson to learn – that snakes are more dignified and impressive than men.

Lawrence wrote many poems of this kind (in a collection called *Birds, Beasts and Flowers,* 1923) and I don't want to claim too much for this one alone. But it does illustrate well the new kind of knowledge that Huxley found in Lawrence's response to the natural world. To put it at its simplest. Lawrence wanted to establish *a new kind of relationship between man and nature,* and something of that relationship is suggested in his poem.

At this point, you may well want to object. What exactly *is* new about sensitive accounts of the world of nature coupled with the recommendation that we ought to pay it more attention? I hope that this *is* an objection you have begun to formulate. If not, you only need to turn to Section IV of the Course Reader, 'Nature and Romantic Literature' to remind yourself that a special feeling for nature is far from being a peculiar invention of Lawrence's. In one sense, he is a twentieth-century continuer of that Romantic tradition. But he also makes a contribution of his own. Let's see if we can define it more closely. Read the extract in the Reader from Lawrence's autobiographical essay 'Nottingham and the Mining Country' (XXV.7, pp. 387–91), getting the general drift of the argument. Then re-read page 389, and decide whether that in itself doesn't give a clue about the special relationship Lawrence thinks we ought to have with natural beauty.

DISCUSSION

We'll come to the general argument shortly, but first what about page 389? Here are the sentences I had in mind.

> Now the love of flowers is a very misleading thing. Most women love flowers as possessions, and as trimmings. They can't look at a flower, and wonder a moment, and pass on. If they see a flower that arrests their attention they must at once pick it, pluck it. Possession! A possession! Something added on to *me*! And most of the so-called love of flowers today is merely this reaching out of possession and egoism: something I've *got*: something that embellishes *me*. Yet I've seen many a collier stand in his back garden looking down at a flower with that odd, remote sort of contemplation which shows a *real* awareness of the presence of beauty. It would not even be admiration, or joy, or delight, or any of those things which so often have a root in the possessive instinct. It would be a sort of contemplation: which shows the incipient artist.

Putting aside the polemics about women, Lawrence's crucial point lies in what he says about the two different ways of admiring the flowers. One is possessive; the other outgoing. One absorbs the natural world into the human world of possessions, making it yet another extension of the ego; the other admires it for what it is – in and for itself. The wondering contemplation Lawrence noticed in the colliers is the same quality evoked in him by the snake, and less elaborately in the description of the snowy Derbyshire scene, where the men almost disappear into the landscape. What Lawrence disliked about a conventional admiration of nature was that it was anthropocentric, nature seen in its relation to man. He wanted to reverse the priorities, and make man see himself in relation to nature. There are touches of this in Romantic poetry, in Wordsworth especially. But for Lawrence it is a constant emphasis.

I don't, of course, know how you reacted to that paragraph about the collier's sense of beauty. Perhaps you thought, 'Well, why shouldn't people take possession of natural beauty? Why not pick the flowers and make this harmless human use of them?' In another mood, Lawrence might have agreed with you. But in this essay, his deeper argument concerns the long process that we call 'industrialization' whereby in the last 150 years, men have achieved – what used to be called without a hint of misgiving – 'the *mastery* of nature'. But Lawrence's misgivings are profound. His writings about nature, whether in essays, poems or as 'the principal personage of his novels' (as Huxley puts it), express deep alarm at this shift in the power balance. He is not just saying, as the first generation of Romantics said, that the natural world is attractive and exerts a healthy influence on humanity at every level. What he is saying is that men's *domination* of the natural world, as expressed in industrial technology and in the scientific analyses that underly it, has dangerous consequences. The specific dangers that he foresees are not, certainly, those we have learned to live with in the last thirty odd years. He concentrates more on the possible damage men do themselves by abstracting themselves from the natural world. Prominent among these dangers is a loss of sanity in the definition of what men take to be valuable human goals. Lawrence foresaw and forewarned against what we have come to know as the fetish of endlessly 'increased productivity', with its inevitable consequence, a more and more extensive exploitation of natural resources. In the extract from 'Nottingham and the Mining Country' printed in the Reader, he attacks the results of nineteenth century indifference to a whole range of human values in terms of the sprawling ugliness of industrial villages like his native Eastwood. In another essay, 'Climbing down Pisgah', he expresses a more radical objection, seeing the wild places of the world everywhere littered with the discarded tin-cans of industrial civilization, much like Ruskin's nightmare of a wholly industrialized England. He shares with nineteenth-century thinkers a revulsion from a mechanistic universe, meaning like them not the presence of industrial machinery as such, but the acceptance of a mechanical conception of human life. At the end of his novel *The Rainbow* (1915), the heroine goes for a walk on the Sussex downs:

> Below she saw the villages and the woods of the weald, and the train running bravely, a gallant little thing, running with all the importance of the world over the water meadows and into the gap of the downs, waving its white steam, yet all the while so little. So little, yet its courage carried it from end to end of the earth, till there was no place it did not go. Yet the downs, in magnificant indifference, bearing limbs and body to the sun, drinking sunshine and sea-wind and sea-wet cloud into its golden skin, with superb stillness and calm of being, was not the downs still more wonderful? The blind, pathetic, energetic courage of the train as it steamed tinily away through the patterned levels to the sea's dimness, so fast and energetic, made her weep. Where was it going? It was going nowhere, it was just going. So blind, so without goal or aim, yet so hasty! She sat on an old prehistoric earthwork and cried, and the tears ran down her face. The train had tunnelled all the earth, blindly, and uglily.

The train of industrialization is gallant, courageous, determined, impressively successful, achieving wonder all over the earth. But where, in the end, was it going? That is the nub of Lawrence's prophetic question of fifty years ago.

ACKNOWLEDGEMENTS

Grateful acknowledgement is made to the following for permission to reproduce material in this unit:

'Challenge to Atomic Power Averted' in *Labour Weekly*, 7 October 1977; P. Larkin 'Going, Going' in *High Windows*, Copyright © 1974 Philip Larkin. Reprinted with the permission of Faber and Faber Ltd. and Farrar, Straus and Giroux Inc. N.Y.; D. H. Lawrence 'Snake' in *The Complete Poems of D. H. Lawrence*, (ed. J. Reeves) Heinemann William Books Ltd. 1967, and Viking Press Inc. New York. Reproduced by permission of Laurence Pollinger Ltd and the Estate of Mrs Frieda Lawrence Ravagli.

A101 AN ARTS FOUNDATION COURSE

1–2A	AN INTRODUCTION TO THE STUDY OF THE HUMANITIES
2B and 9	USES AND ABUSES OF ARGUMENT
3–5	INTRODUCTION TO HISTORY The Significance of History Primary Sources The Writing of History
6–8	INTRODUCTION TO LITERATURE *A Midsummer Night's Dream* Reading Poetry
10–12	INTRODUCTION TO MUSIC Introduction to Music The Case Studies
13–15	INTRODUCTION TO PHILOSOPHY Subjectivity and Scepticism Subjectivity and Value Judgements Scepticism and Sense-Data
16–18	INTRODUCTION TO ART What is Art? What is Art History? Invention and Convention Art and Visual Perception. Form and Meaning
19 and 20	THE RELIGIOUS PERSPECTIVE AFRICAN RELIGIONS

ARTS AND SOCIETY IN AN AGE OF INDUSTRIALIZATION

21	KEY CONCEPTS
22–23	NATURE, WORK AND ART
24–25	THE EXPERIENCE OF INDUSTRIALIZATION
26–27	*JANE EYRE*
28–29	WORK, MORALITY AND HUMAN NATURE
30–31	FROM LISZT TO MUSIC HALL
32	TWENTIETH-CENTURY RESPONSES TO INDUSTRIALIZATION